Current
CONTROVERSIES

Capital Punishment

DATE DUE

Other Books in the Current Controversies Series

Capital Punishment

Paul G. Connors, Book Editor

GREENHAVEN PRESS

An imprint of Thomson Gale, a part of The Thomson Corporation

Detroit • New York • San Francisco • New Haven, Conn. • Waterville, Maine • London

THOMSON

———✶———™

GALE

Christine Nasso, *Publisher*
Elizabeth Des Chenes, *Managing Editor*

© 2007 Gale Group

Star logo is a trademark and Gale and Greenhaven Press are registered trademarks used herein under license.

For more information, contact:
Greenhaven Press
27500 Drake Rd.
Farmington Hills, MI 48331-3535
Or you can visit our Internet site at http://www.gale.com

Articles in Greenhaven Press anthologies are often edited for length to meet page require-ments. In addition, original titles of these works are changed to clearly present the main thesis and to explicitly indicate the author's opinion. Every effort is made to ensure that Greenhaven Press accurately reflects the original intent of the authors. Every effort has been made to trace the owners of copyrighted material.

Cover photograph reproduced by permission of Gstar.

LIBRARY OF CONGRESS CATALOGING-IN-PUBLICATION DATA

Capital punishment / Paul G. Connors, editor.
   p. cm. -- (Current controversies)
   Includes bibliographical references and index.
   ISBN-13: 978-0-7377-3711-0 (hardcover)
   ISBN-13: 978-0-7377-3712-7 (pbk.)
   1. Capital punishment--United States. 2. Capital punishment--Moral and ethical aspects--United States. I. Connors, Paul G.
   KF9227.C2C347 2007
   345.73'0773--dc22

                                                                2007025898

ISBN-10: 0-7377-3711-5 (hardcover)
ISBN-10: 0-7377-3712-3 (pbk.)

Printed in the United States of America
10 9 8 7 6 5 4 3 2 1

Contents

Chapter 1: Is Capital Punishment Ethical?

Yes: Capital Punishment Is Ethical

Chapter 2: Is Capital Punishment Administered Fairly?

Chapter 3: Is Capital Punishment an Effective Deterrent to Crime?

Yes: Capital Punishment Is an Effective Deterrent to Crime

No: Capital Punishment Is Not an Effective
Deterrent to Crime

Chapter 4: Should Capital Punishment Be Abolished or Reformed?

Foreword

By definition, controversies are "discussions of questions in which opposing opinions clash" (Webster's Twentieth Century Dictionary Unabridged). Few would deny that controversies are a pervasive part of the human condition and exist on virtually every level of human enterprise. Controversies transpire between individuals and among groups, within nations and between nations. Controversies supply the grist necessary for progress by providing challenges and challengers to the status quo. They also create atmospheres where strife and warfare can flourish. A world without controversies would be a peaceful world; but it also would be, by and large, static and prosaic.

The Series' Purpose

The purpose of the Current Controversies series is to explore many of the social, political, and economic controversies dominating the national and international scenes today. Titles selected for inclusion in the series are highly focused and specific. For example, from the larger category of criminal justice, Current Controversies deals with specific topics such as police brutality, gun control, white collar crime, and others. The debates in Current Controversies also are presented in a useful, timeless fashion. Articles and book excerpts included in each title are selected if they contribute valuable, long-range ideas to the overall debate. And wherever possible, current information is enhanced with historical documents and other relevant materials. Thus, while individual titles are current in focus, every effort is made to ensure that they will not become quickly outdated. Books in the Current Controversies series will remain important resources for librarians, teachers, and students for many years.

In addition to keeping the titles focused and specific, great care is taken in the editorial format of each book in the series. Book introductions and chapter prefaces are offered to provide background material for readers. Chapters are organized around several key questions that are answered with diverse opinions representing all points on the political spectrum. Materials in each chapter include opinions in which authors clearly disagree as well as alternative opinions in which authors may agree on a broader issue but disagree on the possible solutions. In this way, the content of each volume in Current Controversies mirrors the mosaic of opinions encountered in society. Readers will quickly realize that there are many viable answers to these complex issues. By questioning each author's conclusions, students and casual readers can begin to develop the critical thinking skills so important to evaluating opinionated material.

Current Controversies is also ideal for controlled research. Each anthology in the series is composed of primary sources taken from a wide gamut of informational categories including periodicals, newspapers, books, U.S. and foreign government documents, and the publications of private and public organizations. Readers will find factual support for reports, debates, and research papers covering all areas of important issues. In addition, an annotated table of contents, an index, a book and periodical bibliography, and a list of organizations to contact are included in each book to expedite further research.

Perhaps more than ever before in history, people are confronted with diverse and contradictory information. During the Persian Gulf War, for example, the public was not only treated to minute-to-minute coverage of the war, it was also inundated with critiques of the coverage and countless analyses of the factors motivating U.S. involvement. Being able to sort through the plethora of opinions accompanying today's major issues, and to draw one's own conclusions, can be a complicated and frustrating struggle. It is the editors' hope that Current Controversies will help readers with this struggle.

Introduction

"The death penalty is popular with the American people, although long-term trends suggest support is eroding."

Americans have been debating the merits of capital punishment for four hundred years, and it still provokes many of the same questions that it did four hundred years ago. The first person to be executed in the American colonies was Captain George Kendall in 1608 in the Jamestown colony of Virginia. Kendall, an important member of the colonial governing council, was shot for being a spy for Spain. The circumstances surrounding the execution are not exactly clear, but the incident raises important questions. Is treason a morally justified reason to kill a human being? Was the punishment applied fairly for Kendall, who was suspected of being a Roman Catholic? At the time, Great Britain, a powerful Protestant nation, was anxious about the growing military might of the Catholic powers of Spain and France, both of whom were challenging English efforts to dominate the New World.

Another key consideration: Is capital punishment an effective crime deterrent? In 1612 Virginia governor Sir Thomas Dale enacted the Divine, Moral, and Martial Laws, which, among other things, sanctioned the death penalty for stealing grapes and killing chickens. Modern-day sensibilities hold that capital punishment is too severe for such seemingly minor offenses. However, one has be mindful that in colonial times life and death often revolved around the availability of sustenance, and therefore stealing edibles could result in grave consequences. From this perspective, the Virginia death penalty statutes probably served as an effective deterrent to thievery of foodstuffs. Over the ensuing centuries, as the United States became ethnically, racially, and economically more diverse, other related considerations arose. Opponents of the death penalty contend that the grisly practice is applied unfairly against minorities, the poor, and males. Advocates counter that these segments of society commit the largest number of capital offenses. Opponents also argue that death penalty cases are far more expensive than a lifetime of imprisonment. In contrast, advocates believe that justice cannot be crudely measured in dollars and cents.

According to the Death Penalty Information Center (DPIC), there were 15,555 persons executed in the United States and its colonial predecessors between 1608 and March 2007. Over the seventeenth, eighteenth, and nineteenth centuries, capital punishment gradually rose and peaked at almost 200 executions annually in the mid-1930s. From 1967 to 1977, there was a sharp decline in executions. This was primarily because capital punishment was suspended in 1972 by the U. S. Supreme Court in *Furman v. Georgia* (408 U.S. 238). In this case, the court ruled that many death penalty cases were unconstitutional on the grounds that the death penalty was cruel and unusual punishment in violation of the Eight Amendment to the U.S. Constitution. In 1976 the Supreme Court, in *Gregg v. Georgia* (428 U.S. 153), reauthorized the death penalty. Since this decision, the numbers of condemned inmates have steadily risen. From 1976 to the present, 1,066 people have been executed. Texas is the leader in state executions with 387, followed by Virginia (98), Georgia (39), and Pennsylvania (3). Of those executed since 1976, the DPIC reports that 57 percent (607) were white, 34 percent (363) were black, and 6 percent (72) were Hispanic. The U.S. Census Bureau's *Current Population Surveys* show that whites comprise 77 percent of the population, blacks 13 percent, and Hispanics 6 percent. Twelve states do not have death penalty statutes, and five others have not executed anyone since 1976.

Today there are five legal methods of execution in the United States: hanging, lethal injection, firing squad, cyanide gas (gas chamber), and electrocution. Death by hanging was the primary mode of execution prior to the 1890s. Currently only Delaware and Washington permit it, although both employ lethal injection as an alternative method. Hanging involves weighing the inmate the day before the execution so that a practice execution using a sandbag of the same weight can be conducted. The execution occurs when a trapdoor is opened, the inmate falls through, and the inmate's neck quickly fractures. Idaho is the only state that will authorize the use of a firing squad. The state, which also permits lethal injection, allowed the firing squad as recently as 1996 at the request of the condemned individual. Typically, the hooded inmate is bound to a chair with leather straps, and the chair is surrounded with sandbags. The five-member firing squad is armed with .30 caliber rifles; one member has blank rounds. The squad fires at the inmate's heart. Death is instantaneous.

Five states use cyanide gas, and each has lethal injection as an alternative method. Execution by cyanide gas takes place when the inmate is placed in an airtight chamber and strapped to a chair, under which is a pail of sulfuric acid. When sodium cyanide is released into the pail, a lethal chemical reaction occurs. As the inmate inhales, his or her eyes pop, the skin turns purple, and death occurs. Nebraska is the only state to use electrocution as the sole method of execution. The inmate is shaved, strapped to a chair, and a metal skullcap-shaped electrode, positioned on top of a saltwater-soaked sponge, is connected to the scalp and forehead. A thirty-second jolt of between 500 and 2000 volts is applied. The procedure is repeated until the inmate is dead. Thirty-seven states use lethal injection as a method of execution. The inmate is tied to a table, and a needle is inserted intravenously. The inmate is first injected with a sleep-inducing anesthetic, then a paralyzing agent that stops the inmate's breathing. Death occurs when a third chemical prevents the heart from beating.

The death penalty is popular with the American people, although long-term trends suggest support is eroding. In 2005 the Gallup Poll found that 67 percent favored the death penalty. However, support is significantly lower than it was in 1994 when 80 percent favored the death penalty. When the public was asked in 2006 to choose between the death penalty or life imprisonment with no possibility of parole, 47 percent favored the death penalty and 48 percent chose life imprisonment. In contrast, in 1985, 56 percent favored the death penalty and 34 percent preferred life imprisonment. Interestingly, although support for the death penalty is diminishing, people increasingly believe that it is fairly applied. In 2006, 60 percent of those polled believed that the death penalty was applied fairly, and 35 percent believed it was applied unfairly. Five years earlier, 51 percent believed it was applied fairly, and 41 percent believed it was applied unfairly.

With the possible exception of abortion, no other topic evokes passionate discourse like capital punishment. In the following chapters, two authors share their personal experiences with the contentious practice. Not surprisingly, each views the death penalty differently. The one who lost a loved one in a senseless murder favors retributive justice. The former prison chaplain, on the other hand, who has looked into the hearts of the condemned, believes in the spirit of relentless love and redemption. Other authors approach the topic with cooly reasoned legalistic and statistical analysis. Each viewpoint is nevertheless earnestly argued. Some contend that statistical analyses prove that capital punishment is an effective deterrent, while others maintain that these studies are fraught with technical and conceptual errors. In this volume the debate over capital punishment is framed by the following important questions: Is capital punishment ethical? Is capital punishment administered fairly? Is capital punishment an effective deterrent to crime? Should capital punishment be abolished or reformed? These are not easy questions, therefore readers are provided with no easy answers.

CHAPTER 1

Is Capital Punishment Ethical?

Chapter Preface

Over the years, numerous nongovernmental organizations and the United Nations have attempted to monitor the application of the death penalty across the planet. This task is very difficult, because many of the countries that impose the death penalty are totalitarian regimes. Their use of capital punishment is cloaked in secrecy for they do not provide official and accurate statistics. For example, China probably executes more people than the rest of the world combined. However, the authoritarian government does not offer statistics on executions, death sentencing, or death row populations. According to Human Rights Research (HRR), an independent Canadian human rights consulting service, China executes unofficially somewhere between 1,700 and 8,000 people annually. It is possible that even the Chinese government does not know how many prisoners are awaiting executions nationwide. HRR believes that it is unlikely that China has a centralized registry of death sentences and dispositions.

Amnesty International estimates that at least 5,186 individuals were sentenced to death in fifty-three countries in 2005. That year, the group estimates that 94 percent of all known executions took place in China. Iran executed ninety-four people; Saudi Arabia, eighty-six people; and the United States, sixty people. Opponents of the death penalty often point out that the United States keeps some unsavory company regarding this practice. Nevertheless, unlike those despotic nations, the United States is an open society and every facet of the death penalty is public information, is freely discussed, and is litigated. Moreover, unlike these nondemocratic countries, the United States does not use the death penalty as a tool for political or religious oppression. Capital punishment is reserved for those who commit premeditated murder, espionage, or treason. In contrast, China dispenses the death penalty for human trafficking and serious cases of political corruption. In many Islamic countries, death penalty crimes include adultery, homosexuality, sodomy, and for renouncing Islam. Also, the methods of execution in Islamic countries include beheading, stoning, and stabbing. The United States does not use these brutal methods of execution.

Although the death penalty is legal in the United States in thirty-eight states, it is practiced and supported for the most part in the South. Of the twelve states without the death penalty, none is located in this region. According to the historian Stuart Banner, it is no coincidence that the South and the death penalty are so closely intertwined. Capital punishment's popularity in Dixie is a legacy of slavery. During the nineteenth century, a movement to reform the death penalty swept through the North, permitting execution for no offense other than murder and treason. This trend toward limiting the use of the death penalty continues in the North to this day. In the South, however, the reform movement was much more racially selective. Capital punishment was only imposed on whites convicted of murder, but it applied to blacks for lesser crimes such as attempted murder, rape, attempted rape, arson, and burglary.

Currently the death penalty is only regularly practiced in Texas, Oklahoma, and Virginia. California, Florida, Ohio, Arkansas, Delaware, South Dakota, and Missouri have put the death penalty on hold because of ethical concerns over the supposed inhumane aspects of lethal injection. Illinois is in its seventh year of an open-ended moratorium on executions, and New Jersey is considering its repeal. The Death Penalty Information Center (DPIC) reports that the number of death penalty sentences in 2006 fell to the lowest level in thirty years, reflecting growing ethical worries over the validity of capital convictions.

When a Loved One Is Murdered, the Death Penalty Seems Moral

Olga Polites

Olga Polites is a New Jersey schoolteacher.

I was the one who was home on that Tuesday afternoon in 2000, just having gotten back from a jog. Since my husband was walking in the door from work, I was the one who answered the phone when my sister-in-law called to tell us that her 22-year-old cousin had been brutally murdered in a robbery attempt gone awry. Nearly hysterical, she kept repeating, "We've lost him. We've lost him." After the young men suspected of the crime were arrested the next day, my husband turned to me and asked, "Are you still opposed to capital punishment?"

Since then I've thought a great deal about the death penalty. It's hard not to, and not just because a heinous crime hit so close to home. More recently, lawyers, politicians and even Supreme Court justices are increasingly questioning the role of the death penalty in our justice system. I always thought I knew exactly where I stood on this issue, but now I find myself constantly wavering.

The Murder of Constantine

My husband's cousin Constantine was living at home while attending Temple University when his newly moved-in next-door neighbors and their friend broke into a second-floor bedroom window, looking for some quick cash. Constantine, who didn't have any classes scheduled that day, most likely confronted them. After what police believe was a short struggle, Constantine was tied up with an electrical cord, stabbed 41 times and shot three times in the head. One of the bullets landed in the kitchen sink on the first floor. When his mother came home from work later that afternoon, she found him. Neighbors said her screams could be heard blocks away.

Going to the funeral, watching Constantine's parents deal with the aftermath of what had been done to their son, was terribly painful. For months they couldn't resume working, saying repeatedly that they couldn't think about the future because as far as they were concerned, theirs had abruptly ended.

When the trial took place two years later, all three suspects were convicted, and the prosecutor's office sought the death penalty for the shooter. I was in court for the penalty phase, and as I listened to witnesses testify on his behalf, I was surprised at how indifferent I was to his personal plight. I didn't much care that his family had escaped from Vietnam and that he'd had problems assimilating to American culture, or that his parents had a difficult time keeping him out of trouble.

Personal involvement with the horrible crime of murder renders the academic arguments for or against capital punishment meaningless.

No Extenuating Circumstances

Before this happened, I likely would have argued that this young defendant had extenuating circumstances beyond his control. But not anymore. Maybe it's because my daughter is almost the same age as Constantine was when he was killed, or maybe it's because the reality of experience trumps theoretical beliefs. Whatever the reason, when I looked at the young man sitting at the defense table, I didn't see a victim. All I saw was the man who took my family member's life.

I find it hard now to resist the urge to support the death penalty, especially since it's getting so much attention. Some states, such as Illinois, have placed moratoriums on executions; others have looked into how well defendants are represented at trial. I recognize that there are sound reasons for doing so. The recent use of DNA has proved that some former death-row inmates were unfairly convicted. Locking up the innocent is unacceptable; executing the innocent is unconscionable. And I agree with recent Supreme Court rulings barring the execution of the mentally retarded, the criminally insane and those who committed crimes when they were juveniles.

Perhaps a serious review in the way the death penalty is administered will bring about changes that are clearly necessary. [U.S. Supreme Court] Justice John Paul Stevens is right: there are serious flaws in how we apply capital punishment. Intellectually, I can make the argument that it does not deter crime, and that race and class play major roles in determining who ends up on death row. But the truth is that personal involvement with the horrible crime of murder renders the academic arguments for or against capital punishment meaningless. It was easy to have moral objections to an issue that didn't affect me directly.

The jury verdict for Constantine's killer was life in prison without parole. Although he'll die in jail, there's a part of me that wishes he got the death penalty. I'm not proud of this, nor am I sure that next year, or even next month, I'll feel this way. What I am sure of is that today, my head still says that capital punishment should be abolished, but my heart reminds me of the pain of losing Constantine.

Death by Lethal Injection Is Not Cruel and Unusual Punishment

Cal Thomas

Cal Thomas is America's most widely syndicated op-ed columnist. His column appears in 540 newspapers in the United States and abroad.

Which of the following scenarios constitutes cruel and unusual punishment, as prohibited by the Eighth Amendment to the Constitution: (1) aborting a baby with a fully developed nervous system and probably inflicting great pain; (2) murdering a nightclub manager in cold blood; (3) taking 34 minutes—twice the normal time—to execute the murderer of the nightclub manager?

Anti-death penalty forces want us to believe number three. They claim the Dec. 13 [2006] execution in Florida of Angel Nieves Diaz took too long and required a second injection, thus, violating the Eight Amendment. Florida's outgoing governor, Jeb Bush, has suspended all executions in his state pending an investigation into the state's lethal-injection process. In California, U.S. District Judge Jeremy D. Fogel declared California's execution procedure unconstitutional and lethal injections—the preferred execution method in 37 states—an offense to the ban on cruel and unusual punishment.

One wishes such considerations were available to relatives of the deceased, and to the deceased, themselves, who are not given a choice in the method of their execution, much less the option of continuing to live. Diaz spent more than two decades in prison before he was executed. That probably inflicted cruel and unusual punishment on the relatives of his victim.

'Original intent' of the Founders is important to consider, because what they meant by the phrase and what we think we believe about it differs considerably.

Before too much blood spills from "bleeding heart liberals," it might be helpful to look at Mr. Diaz's criminal resume. According to court records, Diaz was convicted of second-degree murder in his native Puerto Rico. He escaped from prison there and also from Connecticut's Hartford Correctional Center in 1981. In Hartford, he held one guard at knifepoint while another was beaten. Diaz was responsible for three other inmates escaping with him.

Redefining of Cruel and Unusual Punishment

As to the constitutional issue regarding cruel and unusual punishment, here too, some history may be helpful. This is why "original intent" of the Founders is important to consider, because what they meant by the phrase and what we think we believe about it differs considerably.

At the time the Bill of Rights was written, the authors specifically sought to ban such execution methods as burning at the stake, crucifixion and breaking on the wheel. In modern times, the Supreme Court has decided cases that redefine what the Founders meant. In *Hudson v. McMillan* (1992), the Court ruled that the use of excessive physical force against a prisoner might constitute cruel and unusual punishment, even if a prisoner does not suffer serious pain. But the actual infliction of physical pain or hardship is not necessary for such a finding. As far back as 1958, the Supreme Court ruled in *Trop v.*

Dulles that the use of denationalization (the deprivation of citizenship) is a punishment barred by the Eighth Amendment.

To avoid . . . legal hair-splitting, why not return to an earlier and acceptable method of execution that ensures justice is done and inflicts minimal pain on the guilty: the firing squad.

Aside from the period between 1967 and 1976, when capital punishment was effectively suspended, the Supreme Court has consistently ruled that the death penalty does not violate the Eighth Amendment, but that some applications of it might. The Court declared the execution of the mentally retarded to be cruel and unusual punishment and, thus, barred by the Eighth Amendment (*Atkins v. Virginia*, 2002). In *Roper v. Simmons* (2005), the Court ruled it was cruel and unusual punishment to put to death anyone who was under the age of 18 at the time they committed their crime.

Possible Impact on Abortion Law

I don't know how you define cruel and unusual in a lethal injection case. Angel Nieves Diaz was said to have a physical condition that required more drugs to kill him than if he had not had the condition. If those administering the drugs had known about it and given him a double dose so he might die within the "norms" of such executions, would that have been constitutionally acceptable? Does this not get us into the same arbitrary standards that are applied to the unborn? At first, the Supreme Court imposed an arbitrary trimester standard, forbidding the state from restricting a woman's decision in the first three months. But subsequent rulings have resulted in abortion on demand, for any or no reason and at any time.

Will the same erosion of justice against convicted killers mimic the erosion of rights for the unborn innocent? The arbitrary way in which we approach anything of importance today would suggest it might.

To avoid this legal hair-splitting, why not return to an earlier and acceptable method of execution that ensures justice is done and inflicts minimal pain on the guilty: the firing squad.

Juvenile Executions Should Be Ruled Constitutional

Robert H. Bork

Robert H. Bork is a senior fellow at the Hudson Institute and a professor at Ave Maria School of Law.

There are plenty of reasons to deplore *Roper v. Simmons* [2005], the Supreme Court's decision that a murderer under the age of 18 when he committed his crime cannot be given the death penalty. The Court majority once more exhibited for all to see that dazzling combination of lawlessness and moral presumption which increasingly characterizes its Bill of Rights jurisprudence.

The opinion starts unpromisingly, informing us that by "protecting even those convicted of heinous crimes, the Eighth Amendment reaffirms the duty of the government to respect the dignity of all persons." Readers may wonder about the dignity of the victim. Christopher Simmons, then 17, discussed with two companions his desire to murder someone, saying they could "get away with it" because they were minors. He and a juvenile confederate broke into the house of Shirley Crook, covered her eyes and mouth, and bound her hands with duct tape. They drove her to a state park, walked her onto a bridge, tied her hands and feet together with electrical wire, completely covered her whole face with duct tape, and threw her into the Meramec River, where, helpless, she drowned. Simmons bragged about the killing to friends, telling them he had killed a woman "because the bitch seen my face." Arrested, he confessed, and was sentenced to death.

The Supreme Court, though conceding that retribution and deterrence are valid functions of the death penalty, intoned that "we have established the propriety and affirmed the necessity of referring to 'the evolving standards of decency that mark the progress of a maturing society' to determine which punishments are so disproportionate as to be cruel and unusual." That means the justices' views evolve, which is, by definition, progress. Justice Anthony Kennedy's opinion attempted to mask this unpalatable reality by claiming that the meaning of the Eighth Amendment had changed owing to a new "national consensus" against executing under-18 killers. This assertion of a "national consensus," however, was derived from the example of just 18 states that had faced the issue of granting an exemption to juvenile murderers out of the 38 with the death penalty. This dubious escalator means that the founders who allowed such punishments fall well short of our superior understanding of decency, as do the 20 states that today permit the execution of those younger than 18. In Simmons's case, it took the Missouri legislature, the governor, a unanimous jury, and a judge to bring him to death row. All now stand branded, five to four, as morally indecent. The majority did not, and could not, explain why any state is forbidden to make a policy choice—denied its constitutional sovereignty—because other states disagree with it.

The most ominous aspect of Roper *. . . is the Court majority's reliance upon foreign decisions and unratified treaties.*

Trying its hand at psychology, the *Roper* majority argued that neither deterrence nor retribution supported the death penalty for killers under the age of 18. As for deterrence, the Court said, the likelihood that teenagers engage in cost-benefit analysis that attaches any weight to the possibility of execution is so remote as to be virtually non-existent. This in a case where the murderer counted on his minority to "get away with it." This from a Court that finds teenage girls sufficiently mature to decide on abortion without parental knowledge or consent. Retribution was discounted on the theory that young killers, apparently without exception, are less culpable than presumably more thoughtful adult murderers. The Court ignored the fact that juries, unlike the Court, do not decide such issues categorically but by evaluation of the individual and must take youth into account as one mitigating factor.

Retribution was also ruled out without considering its indispensable role in the criminal-justice system. The mixture of reprobation and expiation in retribution is sometimes required as a dramatic mark of our sense of great evil and to reinforce our respect for ourselves and the dignity of others. None of this was examined by the Court. Its steady piecemeal restriction of the death penalty—now "reserved for a narrow category of crimes and offenders"—suggests that the Court is on a path to abolish capital punishment altogether even though the Constitution four times explicitly assumes its legitimacy.

The most ominous aspect of *Roper*, however, is the Court majority's reliance upon foreign decisions and unratified treaties. The opinion cited "the stark reality that the United States is the only country in the world that continues to give official sanction to the juvenile death penalty," a fact the Court found "instructive" in interpreting the American Constitution. Since the nations of Europe have, among others, abolished the death penalty, the Court seems to be suggesting that we (or rather the justices) should do likewise. After all, "[w]e have previously recognized the relevance of the views of the international community in determining whether a punishment is cruel and unusual." If the meaning of a document over 200 years old can be affected by the current state of world opinion, James Madison and his colleagues labored in vain.

Article 37 of the United Nations Convention on the Rights of the Child, we are reminded, expressly prohibits capital punishment for those under 18. The United States—almost uniquely among countries—did not ratify it. Indeed, this country has never accepted any international covenant containing the prohibition in Article 37. "In sum, it is fair to say that the United States now stands alone in a world that has turned its face against the juvenile death penalty." To accept such covenants would, of course, be attempting to alter our Constitution by treaty. Perhaps that is why the Court hedged: "The opinion of the world community, while not controlling our outcome, does provide respected and significant confirmation for our own conclusions." This "underscores the centrality of those same rights within our own heritage of freedom." That comes pretty close to accepting foreign control of the American Constitution.

American self-government and sovereignty would be submerged in a web of international regulations.

What is really alarming about *Roper* and other cases citing foreign law (six justices now engage in that practice) is that the Court, in tacit coordination with foreign courts, is moving toward a global bill of rights. Neither our courts nor the foreign courts are bound by actual constitutions. Prof. Lino Graglia was quite right when he said that "the first and most important thing to know about American constitutional law is that it has virtually nothing to do with the Constitution." That is certainly the case with the Bill of Rights. From abortion to homosexual sodomy, from religion to political speech and pornography, from capital punishment to discrimination on the basis of race and sex, the Court is steadily remaking American political, social, and cultural life. As Justice Antonin Scalia once said in dissent, "Day by day, case by case, [the Court] is busy designing a Constitution for a country I do not recognize."

The courts of the United Kingdom, Canada, Israel, and almost all Western countries are doing the same thing, replacing the meaning of their charters with their own preferences. Nor are these judicial alterations random. The culture war evident in the United States is being waged internationally, both within individual nations and in international institutions and tribunals. It is a war for dominance between two moral visions of the future. One is the liberal-elite preference for radical personal autonomy and the other is the general public's desire for some greater degree of community and social authority. Elite views are fairly uniform across national boundaries, and since American and foreign judges belong to elites and respond to elite views, judge-made constitutions tend to converge. It hardly matters what particular constitutions say or were understood to mean by those who adopted them.

Judges are not, of course, the only forces for a new elite global morality. Governments and non-governmental organizations are actively promoting treaties, conventions, and new institutions (the International Criminal Court, for example) that embody their view that sovereignty and nation-states are outmoded and that we must move toward regional or even global governance. American self-government and sovereignty would be submerged in a web of international regulations. The Supreme Court, in decisions like *Roper*, adds constitutional law to the web. That is the one strand, given our current acceptance of judicial supremacy, that cannot be rejected democratically. What is clear is that foreign elites understand the importance of having the Supreme Court on their side, which is precisely why their human-rights organizations have begun filing amicus briefs urging our Supreme Court to adopt the foreign, elite view of the American Constitution.

Roper is one more reason that it is urgent that the president nominate and battle for justices who will rein in a Court run amok.

Capital Punishment Is Moral to Prevent the Taking of Innocent Lives

Cass R. Sunstein and Adrian Vermeule

Cass R. Sunstein is a professor of jurisprudence at the University of Chicago Law School, and Adrian Vermeule is a professor of law at the University of Chicago.

Many people believe capital punishment is morally impermissible. In their view, executions are inherently cruel and barbaric. Often they add that capital punishment is not, and cannot be, imposed in a way that adheres to the rule of law. They contend that as administered, capital punishment ensures the execution of (some) innocent people, and also that it reflects arbitrariness, in the form of random or invidious infliction of the ultimate penalty.

Defenders of capital punishment come in two different camps. Some are retributivists. Following [the philospher Immanuel] Kant, they claim that for the most heinous forms of wrongdoing, the penalty of death is morally justified or perhaps even required. Other defenders of capital punishment are consequentialists and often also welfarists. They contend that the deterrent effect of capital punishment is significant and that it justifies the infliction of the ultimate penalty. Consequentialist defenses of capital punishment, however, tend to assume that capital punishment is (merely) morally permissible, as opposed to being morally obligatory.

State Omissions Are Morally Important

Our goal here is to suggest that the debate over capital punishment is rooted in an unquestioned assumption, and that

Cass R. Sunstein and Adrian Vermeule, "Is Capital Punishment Morally Required? The Relevance of Life-Life Tradeoffs," AEI-Brookings Joint Center for Regulatory Studies, March 2005, pp. 1–3, 7–11, 41–42. http://aei-brookings.org. © 2005 by Cass R. Sunstein and Adrian Vermeule. All rights reserved. Reproduced by permission.

the failure to question that assumption is a serious moral error. The assumption is that for governments, acts are morally different from omissions. We want to raise the possibility that an indefensible form of the act-omission distinction is crucial to the most prominent objections to capital punishment—and that defenders of capital punishment, apparently making the same distinction, have failed to notice that on the logic of their theory, capital punishment is morally obligatory, not just permissible. We want to suggest, in other words, that capital punishment may be morally required not for retributive reasons, but in order to prevent the taking of innocent lives.

The foundation for our argument is a large and growing body of evidence that capital punishment may well have a deterrent effect, possibly a quite powerful one.

The suggestion bears not only on moral and political debates, but also on constitutional questions. In invalidating the death penalty for juveniles, for example, the Supreme Court did not seriously engage the possibility that capital punishment for juveniles may help to prevent the death of innocents, including the deaths of juvenile innocents. And if our suggestion is correct, it is connected to many questions outside of the context of capital punishment. If omissions by the state are often indistinguishable, in principle, from actions by the state, then a wide range of apparent failures to act—in the context not only of criminal and civil law, but of regulatory law as well—should be taken to raise serious moral and legal problems. Those who accept our arguments in favor of the death penalty may or may not welcome the implications for government action in general. In many situations, ranging from environmental quality to highway safety to relief of poverty, our arguments suggest that in light of imaginable empirical findings, government is obliged to provide far more protection than it now does, and that it should not be permitted to hide behind unhelpful distinctions between acts and omissions.

Growing Evidence that Capital Punishment Is a Deterrent

The foundation for our argument is a large and growing body of evidence that capital punishment may well have a deterrent effect, possibly a quite powerful one. A leading study suggests that each execution prevents some eighteen murders, on average. The particular numbers do not much matter. If the current evidence is even roughly correct, then a refusal to impose capital punishment will effectively condemn numerous innocent people to death. States that choose life imprisonment, when they might choose capital punishment, are ensuring the deaths of a large number of innocent people. On moral grounds, a choice that effectively condemns large numbers of people to death seems objectionable to say the least. For those who are inclined to be skeptical of capital punishment for moral reasons—a group that includes one of the current authors—the task is to consider the possibility that the failure to impose capital punishment is, prima facie and all things considered, a serious moral wrong. . . .

For many years, the deterrent effect of capital punishment was sharply disputed. But a great deal of recent evidence strengthens the claim that capital punishment has large deterrent effects. The reason for the shift is that a wave of sophisticated econometric studies have exploited a newly-available form of data, so-called "panel data" that uses all information from a set of units (states or counties) and follows that data over an extended period of time. A leading study used county-level panel data from 3,054 U.S. counties between 1977 and 1996. The authors find that the murder rate is significantly reduced by both death sentences and executions. The most striking finding is that on average, each execution results in 18 fewer murders.

Other econometric studies also find a substantial deterrent effect. In two papers, Paul Zimmerman [a senior economist with the Federal Communications Commission] uses state-level panel data from 1978 onwards to measure the deterrent effect of execution rates and execution methods. He estimates that each execution deters an average of fourteen murders. Using state-level data from 1977 to 1997, [H. Naci] Mocan and [R. Kaj] Gittings [economics professors at the University of Colorado at Denver] find that each execution deters five murders on average. They also find that increases in the murder rate come from removing people from death row and also from commutations in death sentences. Yet another study, based on state-level data from 1997–1999, finds that a death sentence deters 4.5 murders and an execution deters three murders. The same study investigates the question whether executions deter crimes of passion and murders by intimates. The answer is clear: these categories of murder are deterred by capital punishment. The deterrent effect of the death penalty is also found to be a function of the length of waits on death row, with a murder deterred for every 2.75 years of reduction in the period before execution.

It hardly seems sensible that governments should ignore evidence demonstrating a significant possibility that a certain step will save large numbers of innocent lives.

In the period between 1972 and 1976, the Supreme Court produced an effective moratorium on capital punishment, and an extensive study exploits that fact to estimate the deterrent effect. Using state-level data from 1960–2000, the authors make before-and-after comparisons, focusing on the murder rate in each state before and after the death penalty was suspended and reinstated. The authors find a substantial deterrent effect. After suspending the death penalty, 91% of states faced an increase in homicides—and in 67% of states, the rate was decreased after reinstatement of capital punishment.

A recent study offers more refined findings. Disaggregating the data on a state by state basis, [economist] Joanna Shepherd finds that the nation-wide deterrent effect of capital punishment is entirely driven by only six states—and that no deterrent effect can be found in the twenty-one other states that have restored capital punishment. What distinguishes the six from the twenty-one? The answer lies in the fact that states showing a deterrent effect are executing more people than states that do not. In fact the data show a "threshold effect": deterrence is found in states that had at least nine executions between 1977 and 1996. In states below that threshold, no deterrence can be found. This finding is intuitively plausible. Unless executions reach a certain level, murderers may act as if the death is so improbable as not to be worthy of concern. Her main lesson is that once the level of executions reaches a certain level, the deterrent effect of capital punishment is substantial.

Governments Should Not Ignore Evidence

All in all, the recent evidence of a deterrent effect from capital punishment seems impressive. But in studies of this kind, it is hard to control for confounding variables, and a degree of doubt inevitably remains. It remains possible that these findings will be exposed as statistical artifacts or will be found to rest on flawed econometric methods. More broadly, skeptics are likely to question the mechanisms by which capital punishment has a deterrent effect. On the skeptical view, many murderers lack a clear sense of the likelihood and perhaps even the existence of executions in their state; further problems for the deterrence claim are introduced by the fact that capital punishment is imposed infrequently and after long delays. In any case many murders are committed in a passionate state that does not lend itself to an all-things-considered analysis on the part of perpetrators. . . .

These suppositions are in some tension with existing evidence. But let us suppose that these doubts are reasonable. If so, should current findings be deemed irrelevant for purposes of policy and law? That would be an odd conclusion. In regulation as a whole, it is common to embrace some version of the Precautionary Principle—the idea that steps should be taken to prevent significant harm even if cause-and-effect relationships remain unclear and even if the risk is not likely to come to fruition. Even if we reject strong versions of the Precautionary Principle, it hardly seems sensible that governments should ignore evidence demonstrating a significant possibility that a certain step will save large numbers of innocent lives.

For capital punishment, critics often seem to assume that evidence on deterrent effects should be ignored if reasonable questions can be raised about it. But as a general rule, this is implausible. In most contexts, the existence of reasonable questions is hardly an adequate reason to ignore evidence of severe harm. If it were, many environmental controls would be in serious jeopardy. We do not mean to suggest that government should commit what many people consider to be, prima facie, a serious moral wrong simply on the basis of speculation that this step will do some good. But a degree of reasonable doubt does not seem sufficient to doom capital punishment, if the evidence suggests that significant deterrence occurs.

If capital punishment does have a strong deterrent effect, there is a crucial implication: it must be the case that capital punishment is not a wholly capricious system of punishment, pervaded by false positives.

In any event, we will proceed by stipulating to the validity of this evidence, in order to isolate the question of its moral significance. Our primary concern here is not to reach a final judgment about the evidence, but how to evaluate capital punishment given the assumption of a substantial deterrent effect. Those who doubt the evidence might ask themselves how they would assess the moral questions if they were ultimately convinced that life-life tradeoffs were actually involved—as, for example, in hostage situations in which officials are authorized to use deadly force to protect the lives of innocent people.

Capital Punishment Has a High Degree of Accuracy

If capital punishment does have a strong deterrent effect, there is a crucial implication: it must be the case that capital punishment is not a wholly capricious system of punishment, pervaded by false positives. At the very least, some or many prospective murderers must believe that the system has a high degree of accuracy. The simple reason is that if capital punishment were thoroughly error-prone and seen as such, the deterrent signal of the punishment would be so diluted that it would be extremely unlikely to produce such strong and consistent empirical traces as those described above. At the limit, if capital punishment were entirely random, falling with utter arbitrariness upon innocent and guilty alike, there would be no reason for any prospective criminal to factor it into calculations about the costs and benefits of crime. . . . Of course it remains undeniable that capital punishment is sometimes imposed erroneously, and undeniable too that it is sometimes imposed arbitrarily or on invidious grounds within the set of guilty defendants. Nothing we say here is meant to suggest that states should be content with erroneous or arbitrary death sentences. But the evidence suggests that there is at least a high degree of accuracy, in the sense of avoiding false positives, in the infliction of capital punishment. . . .

Governments Without Capital Punishment May Be Violating Citizen Rights

We conjecture that something like the following set of views about capital punishment has been and probably still is widespread in the legal academy. Capital punishment does not deter, or at least the evidence that it does so is essentially nonexistent; some categories of murders, especially crimes of passion, are undeterrable (at least by capital punishment); even if capital punishment has a deterrent effect, the effect is marginal, perhaps because of the relatively small number of capital sentences and the long time lags between sentencing and execution; the system of capital punishment is rife with error and arbitrariness.

A government that settles upon a package of crime-control policies that does not include capital punishment might well seem ... to be both violating the rights and reducing the welfare of its citizens.

The recent evidence raises doubts about all of these views. Capital punishment may well have strong deterrent effects; there is evidence that few categories of murders are inherently undeterrable, even so-called crimes of passion; some studies find extremely large deterrent effects; error and arbitrariness undoubtedly occur, but the evidence of deterrence suggests that prospective murderers are receiving a clear signal.

The moral and legal commentary on capital punishment ought to be sensitive to any significant revision in what we know. Life-life tradeoffs are inescapably involved. In light of recent evidence, a government that settles upon a package of crime-control policies that does *not* include capital punishment might well seem, at least prima facie, to be both violating the rights and reducing the welfare of its citizens—just as would a state that failed to enact simple environmental measures promising to save a great many lives.

Capital Punishment May Be Morally Obligatory

The most common basis for resisting this conclusion, and our principal target here, is some version of the distinction between acts and omissions. Opponents of capital punishment frequently appeal to an intuition that intentional killing by the government and its agents is morally objectionable in a way that simply allowing private killings is not. Whatever the general merits of the distinction between acts and omissions in the moral theory of individual conduct, we think it gets little purchase on questions of governmental policy. Government cannot help but act in ways that affect the actions of citizens; where citizens decide whether or not to kill each other in light of government's policies, it is not clear even as a conceptual matter what it would mean for government not to act. For government to adopt a mix of criminal-justice policies that happens not to include capital punishment is not an "omission" or a "failure to act" in any meaningful sense. Likewise, deontological injunctions against unjustified killing, which we have not questioned here, are of little help in these settings. Unjustified killing is exactly what capital punishment prevents.

If the recent evidence of deterrence is shown to be correct, then opponents of capital punishment will face an uphill struggle on moral grounds.

If this argument is correct, it has broad implications, some of which may not be welcomed by advocates of capital punishment. Government engages in countless omissions, many of which threaten people's health and safety; consider the failure to reduce highway fatalities, to regulate greenhouse gas emissions, to prevent domestic violence, to impose further controls on private uses of guns, even to redistribute wealth to those who most need it. Suppose that it is not sensible, in these and other contexts, to characterize government omissions as such, or suppose that even if the characterization is sensible, it lacks moral relevance. If so, then government might well be compelled, on one or another ground, to take steps to protect people against statistical risks, even if those steps impose costs and harms; much will depend on what the facts show.

Any objection to capital punishment, we believe, must rely on something other than abstract injunctions against the taking of life. If the recent evidence of deterrence is shown to be correct, then opponents of capital punishment will face an uphill struggle on moral grounds. If each execution is saving many lives, the harms of capital punishment would have to be very great to justify its abolition, far greater than most critics have heretofore alleged. There is always residual uncertainty in social science and legal policy, and we have attempted to describe, rather than to defend, recent findings here. But if those findings are ultimately shown to be right, capital punishment has a strong claim to being, not merely morally permissible, but morally obligatory, above all from the standpoint of those who wish to protect life.

Capital Punishment Is Simply Murder

Gary Egeberg

Gary Egeberg is a former state prison chaplain, who currently leads workshops and retreats in Minnesota.

When I left the Twin Cities in June 2002 to begin my service as a lay Catholic chaplain in a California maximum security prison housing 5,000 male inmates, I had no idea what to expect other than warmer weather. I certainly didn't expect to find myself changing my position on the death penalty. I didn't expect to go from being against it to being for it. To be honest, I was a little bit embarrassed to find my heart hardening and my mind closing, especially so quickly.

I learned a lot during my three years as a prison chaplain. I learned that many inmates have done absolutely horrendous things, and that a significant number are unable or unwilling to take responsibility for their actions. I also learned that prison is an incredibly hard place to become a better human being because of the violent and fearful nature of the surroundings. And I learned that the fence is pretty darn thin, and that with a slight change in genetic or environmental makeup or with a poor choice here or there, I could just as easily have been a resident in need of a chaplain rather than the one serving as a chaplain.

Favoring the Death Penalty

As a Catholic chaplain, I led weekly Word-Communion services on five yards (each yard functioned as a separate prison housing approximately 1,000 inmates) and once a month accompanied a bilingual priest who came to say Mass and hear confessions. I visited men in the prison hospital and in the "hole" (a prison within the prison for those who are caught selling drugs, fighting and so on). I comforted men who lost loved ones on the outside, and I taught a variety of classes on prayer and forgiveness and personal transformation. I lugged an artificial Christmas tree with me from yard to yard to brighten up our Advent and Christmas services and I led Stations of the Cross services during the season of Lent.

Though I had far more positive experiences with inmates than negative ones, I still found myself to be increasingly for the death penalty. In fact, when my family and I returned to the Twin Cities this past August [2005], I was much more in favor of the death penalty—especially if the state had irrefutable DNA evidence—than against it. Why this shift in position?

Three things took place over the course of several months to change my stance on the death penalty so that I became more deeply against it than I was before I began my prison ministry.

Well, I had met quite a few inmates who had maimed and murdered and who didn't seem to be too concerned about their victims or victims' families. I read many prison files that contained narratives of their trials and disturbing pictures of their victims. It bothered me to see inmates with color televisions in their cells along with all sorts of snack food. I observed inmates happily playing volleyball, soccer, basketball, handball, softball, checkers, chess, dominos and cards, which some of their victims will never have a chance to do again. In short, it didn't seem fair or right that those who had intentionally taken another person's life should be able to enjoy things, much less live.

This was the mindset with which I returned to the Twin Cities. No, I wasn't bitter. I enjoyed my years as a chaplain. I met inmates who had changed for the better and inmates who were in the process of changing for the better. I knew inmates I would be happy to have as next-door neighbors and some I consider to be like brothers. I came to know many inmates who were wonderful, loving Catholics, who cared about those who were suffering in all corners of the world. Yet I came home in favor of the death penalty.

If you want to punish inmates for murder, raise their morality, raise their consciousness, raise their humanity— don't kill them.

Changing Stance on the Death Penalty

But then three things took place over the course of several months to change my stance on the death penalty so that I became more deeply against it than I was before I began my prison ministry.

First, I started to meditate again. I started to get out of my head, out of seeing things through my mind and limited ego, and started to get in touch with my heart. For as [the French writer] Antoine de Saint-Exupery so astutely observed, "It is only with the heart that one can see rightly." One purpose of prayer and meditation is to point out our blindness—which is inevitable when we rely solely on rational thought—and to re-store our heart-sight, the vision with which Jesus saw and continues to see the world. If we Catholics don't pray and meditate, it becomes very easy to see life and complex issues such as capital punishment just the way others in our society do, through the understandable but distorted lens of "an eye for an eye" and "a life for a life." When we pray and meditate, the Holy Spirit gives us the eyes of Jesus, through which we can begin to see that the worst person among us has human dignity and potential for transformation. And that when we can't see this dignity and potential, God can.

Second, in conjunction with prayer and meditation, the words of the Gospel began to penetrate and break up the hardened regions of my heart, especially passages such as: "Love your enemies and pray for those who persecute you, so that you may be children of your Father in heaven; for he makes his sun rise on the evil and on the good, and sends rain on the righteous and on the unrighteous" (Mt 5:44–45). Jesus' vision is that we are all one. Our brokenness keeps us from buying into this vision and living by this unalterable truth. And whatever happens to the least of us, to the victim and the murderer, happens not only to Jesus but to us all. Adding another victim through capital punishment does nothing to contribute to this oneness. Capital punishment is not only murder. It is killing someone who, like you and me, is made in the image of God. Our behavior does not change the fact that we are children of our Creator God and brothers and sisters of Jesus Christ.

Third, I was influenced by some reading I was doing on the stages of moral development. Generally speaking, many inmates are imprisoned within a childish developmental stage dominated by selfishness and an "everything centers around me" approach to life. If you want to punish inmates for murder, raise their morality, raise their consciousness, raise their humanity—don't kill them. Then as they develop as human beings, as they move up the moral ladder, so to speak, they will have true remorse and they will suffer for what they have done to hurt another human being. They will have to live with it. In fact, some transformed inmates will be aghast at what they did. I met at least 20 inmates during my three years who had metamorphosed from being heartless killers to tenderhearted human beings. They have an incredibly hard time forgiving themselves; in fact, many of them can't. They are trying to make a positive contribution, even though they may never see life again outside of prison. I am personally proud of these men and humbled that I had the privilege to come to know them.

It hurts for all of us to become more human, to open our minds and hearts and to have our circles of love expanded. The pain that murderers will suffer as they become more human is a pain that will hurt, but one that will also be redemptive. Jesus came to redeem the world and then passed the job along to us to continue ministering to the brokenness within and around us. When we say no to capital punishment, we are allowing the Spirit of relentless love to continue working in the hearts and minds of those we sometimes want to see pay with their lives. All we have to do is take an honest look at ourselves to see how much room there is for growth in our own journey to holiness and wholeness. And when we realize how far we have come and how far we have to go, we realize that we have no business saying that God cannot help a cold-blooded murderer become more human and holy in God's own way and time.

As the saying goes, "Be patient with me, for God isn't done with me yet." Our heads may say that the death penalty is fair; our Spirit-led hearts know that our God is out to heal all of us, whether we deem it fair or not.

Death by Lethal Injection Is Inhumane

Deborah W. Denno

Deborah W. Denno is a law professor at Fordham University School of Law in New York City.

I am sitting in the witness stand of a courtroom in Frankfort, Kentucky, facing David, a young defense lawyer at Kentucky's Department of Advocacy. David is standing at a podium questioning me. It is April 18, 2005. We have been waiting for this moment for a very long time. I am the first of a dozen expert witnesses to testify in *Baze et al. v. Rees et al.*, a bench trial concerning the constitutionality of Kentucky's lethal injection protocol. Lethal injection is this country's most widely used method of executing death row inmates. I am testifying on behalf of the plaintiffs, Ralph Baze and Thomas Bowling, two condemned inmates who are claiming that the Kentucky protocol constitutes cruel and unusual punishment under the Eighth Amendment of the United States Constitution and Section 17 of the Kentucky Constitution. The three defendants involved in this trial are most responsible for how Kentucky's executions are handled. They are the Commissioner of the Kentucky Department of Corrections, the Warden of the Kentucky State Penitentiary, and the Governor of the Commonwealth of Kentucky.

For months, David and his colleagues have been preparing for this trial. I am here because I have studied lethal injection, indeed all of this country's execution methods, for nearly fifteen years while a professor at Fordham University School of Law in New York City. The topic of execution methods has so troubled me that I have continued to follow it during my entire legal career, in spite of other professional interests and commitments. To me, the problem with execution methods symbolizes nearly everything that has gone astray with the death penalty in this country.

This courtroom scenario in Frankfort is not what people typically think of when they hear the word "trial" in the popularized television sense of that word. Everything about the setting projects smallness and understatement. Frankfort, the state capital, has a population of less than 30,000 people. The city's courthouse is a miniature of all the ones I have ever seen. There are only two courtrooms in the entire building. There is no Starbucks. Most certainly, this is no place for a *Boston Legal* episode where trials seem like packed fish bowls viewed by hundreds. As I sit in this courtroom, however, I am continually reminded that some of the most significant cases ever decided in this country started in locales that many Americans would consider quaint. We merely watch, not experience, *Law & Order* lives. . . .

This 2005 trial in Kentucky brings a fresh message: it is the fullest and most sophisticated investigation of lethal injection ever conducted.

Lethal Injection Is Not What the Public Thinks It Is

Regardless, the "how" of Kentucky's executions is the heart of the plaintiffs' case. The constitutionality of execution methods is also of burgeoning significance throughout the country as medical investigations continually reveal the troubling, and all too latent, aspects of lethal injection. The concern is highly democratic within the death row inmate population. The risks of an inhumane lethal injection affect every inmate equally, no matter their color, their class, the quality of their legal representation or the purported social value of their victim. Each inmate has been designated by the state to die in the same way. In this bench trial, we are wrangling over how exactly that death will occur.

David and I both believe that lethal injection is not what the public and many lawmakers think it is—a serene and soothing way to die, like putting a sick animal to sleep. We think the process is inhumane and tortuous, the result of medical folly, political compromise. We want to convince the Kentucky judge of this. The attorneys representing the Commonwealth of Kentucky want to convince the judge that we are wrong. They claim that lethal injection is in fact a humane and suitable way to die. . . .

In the past few years, there have been a number of evidentiary hearings on lethal injection across the country. From lethal injection's inception in 1977, the method of execution has been continually under constitutional attack. Yet, lawyers have also always had a great deal of difficulty finding out the specifics of how a lethal injection is conducted and what protocols or guidelines have been and are used to ensure that executions are conducted humanely. The lack of information has made it impossible to have a thorough challenge to the method's constitutionality. Over the years, however, a committed group of academics, lawyers, and doctors have chipped away at the shell of secrecy, releasing forward a bounty of new information on a wide range of issues. This 2005 trial in Kentucky brings a fresh message: it is the fullest and most sophisticated investigation of lethal injection ever conducted.

Lethal Injection in Kentucky

In most states, including Kentucky, lethal injection involves having an executioner syringe three chemicals into the body of an inmate sentenced to death: *sodium thiopental*, an "ultrashort" acting barbiturate intended to put the inmate to sleep; *pancuronium bromide*, a paralytic agent used to immobilize the inmate; and *potassium chloride*, a toxin that induces cardiac arrest and hastens the inmate's death. These injections are to occur sequentially, while the inmate is strapped to a gurney, a padded stretcher typically used for transporting hospitalized patients. There have been photos of the execution gurney so artfully shot that the gurney does indeed look like a bed, an inviting place where a person would want to stretch out if not for the fact it is to be used for a killing.

I use the term "death bed" to depict this execution scenario even though these words have not been applied in this context before, either by legal practitioners or academics. Typically, deathbed connotes the last few hours of a dying person's life or the place from which a dying person makes a final statement. An inmate on an executioner's gurney, however, is strapped down, not free, and is dying not because of failed health but because the state has determined the inmate should be punished to death.

Many of the problems with lethal injection could be attributed to vague lethal injection statutes, uninformed prison personnel, and skeletal or inaccurate lethal injection protocols.

Major Study of Lethal Injection Protocols

In 2002, I published an article in a symposium issue of the *Ohio State Law Journal* focusing on the problems associated with lethal injection. The article contended that lethal injection was unconstitutional under the United States Supreme Court's interpretation of the Eighth Amendment's Cruel and Unusual Punishment Clause for a range of reasons: the procedure involved the "unnecessary and wanton infliction of pain," the "risk" of such pain, "physical violence," the offense to "human dignity," and the contravention of "evolving standards of decency."

My conclusions were supported by a large study I conducted of the most up-to-date protocols for administering lethal injection in all thirty-six states, which, at that time, used anesthesia for state executions. The study focused on a number of factors that are critical to conducting a lethal injection humanely, such as: the types and amounts of chemicals that are injected; the selection, training, preparation, and qualifications of the lethal injection team; the involvement of medical personnel; the presence of witnesses, including media witnesses; as well as details on how the procedure is conducted and how much of it witnesses can see. The fact that executions are not typically conducted by doctors, but by execution technicians, is a critical aspect of the process.

In the article, I argued that many of the problems with lethal injection could be attributed to vague lethal injection statutes, uninformed prison personnel, and skeletal or inaccurate lethal injection protocols. When some state protocols provide details, such as the amount and type of chemicals that executioners inject, they often reveal striking errors, omissions, and ignorance about the procedure. Such inaccurate or missing information heightens the likelihood that a lethal injection will be botched and suggests that states are not capable of executing an inmate without violating the prohibition against cruel and unusual punishment.

Lethal Injection Drawbacks

Over the decades, there have been many drawbacks associated with lethal injection, all of which contradict the public's perception that injection is a peaceful way to die. First, evidence suggests that some inmates are given insufficient amounts of the initial chemical, sodium thiopental, and therefore regain consciousness while being injected with the second and third chemicals. In this situation, the inmate will suffer extraordinary pain while the second chemical, pancuronium bromide, takes its paralytic effect, preventing the inmate from moving or communicating in any way. Then when the third chemical, potassium chloride, is administered to cause death, the paralyzed inmate will experience a burning sensation likened to a hot poker inserted into his arm, which spreads over his entire body until it causes the heart to stop. It is striking that the American Veterinary Medical Association has condemned the use of pancuronium bromide and potassium chloride for the euthanasia of animals because the paralyzing effect of the pancuronium bromide would mask the excruciating pain that the animal was experiencing from the potassium chloride. These chemicals are too horrifying for killing animals but they are routinely used to execute human beings.

The vagueness of the protocols also results in executioners often ignoring an inmate's particular physical characteristics (such as age, body weight, drug use), factors that have a major impact on an individual's reactions to chemicals and the condition of their veins. Physicians have problems finding suitable veins for injection among individuals who are diabetic, obese, or extremely muscular. Heavy drug users, who constitute a significant portion of the death row population, present particularly difficult challenges because of their damaged veins and resistance to even high levels of lethal injection chemicals.

It is remarkable . . . that Judge Crittenden states that one part of Kentucky's protocol was indeed unconstitutional.

All of these difficulties are compounded for untrained executioners, who are the ones typically carrying out the protocols. For example, executioners having trouble finding a vein because of obesity or drug use may insert a catheter into a sensitive area of the body, such as a groin or hand. In some cases, if a vein can still not be found, executioners will perform a "cut-down" procedure, which requires an incision to expose the damaged vein. The cut-down procedure is used with disturbing frequency in lethal injection executions, while it is only a memory to modern day anesthesiologists, who have far more feasible alternatives. The cut-down problem has even caught the eye of the Supreme Court. In May 2004, in *Nelson v. Campbell* the Court unanimously held that an Alabama death row inmate could file a civil rights suit to challenge the state's proposal to execute him with a cut-down procedure. *Nelson* is the first case where the Court has addressed the lethal injection issue. While the *Nelson* case did not concern the merits of lethal injection, it appears the Court may have already come to terms with the broader aspects of the procedure because the Court was willing to call into question one aspect of it. . . .

The Ruling

On July 8, 2005, Judge [R.L.] Crittenden released his decision. With one exception, he upheld the constitutionality of Kentucky's lethal injection procedure. I was very disappointed with this outcome, of course. But I also thought the press accounts of this bottom line conclusion belied the details and true significance of all that Judge Crittenden actually wrote. For those of us in the death penalty trenches, a close read of the opinion reveals some extraordinary and unprecedented statements about the flaws of the lethal injection procedure, as well as recommendations for how it should be improved.

It is remarkable, for example, that Judge Crittenden states that one part of Kentucky's protocol was indeed unconstitutional. He held that it was cruel and unusual for the Kentucky protocol to allow Department of Corrections personnel to insert a catheter into the condemned's neck. No judge has ever made such a finding about lethal injection. Judge Crittenden appeared to be particularly influenced by the testimony of a medical doctor with the Kentucky Department of Corrections. That doctor stated that he would refuse to perform the neck injection procedure and that those who would be performing it are insufficiently trained to do so. Judge Crittenden's perspective on this matter is very clear: "The Plaintiffs have demonstrated by a preponderance of the evidence that the procedure where the Department of Corrections attempts to insert an intravenous catheter into the neck through the carotid artery or jugular vein does create a substantial risk of wanton and unnecessary infliction of pain, torture or lingering death."

Judge Crittenden also made novel findings of fact in response to a number of important points raised during the bench hearing that I think will be critical in future litigation on lethal injection, or it should be. . . .

[For example,] the opinion emphasized that there was "scant evidence" that any of the states that have since adopted lethal injection, including Kentucky, engaged in any research on lethal injection to justify their decision to follow Oklahoma's lead. . . .

I did think Judge Crittenden's decision rang of naiveté in some places.

Likewise, Judge Crittenden accentuates the lack of research and study in other aspects involved in the creation of lethal injection protocols. He notes, for instance, that "[t]hose persons assigned the initial task of drafting the [Commonwealth of Kentucky's] first lethal injection protocol were provided with little to no guidance on drafting a lethal injection protocol and were resolved to mirror protocols in other states, namely Indiana, Virginia, Georgia, and Alabama." For example, Department of Corrections personnel "did not conduct any independent or scientific or medical studies or consult any medical professionals concerning the drugs and dosage amounts to be injected into the condemned." Such reluctance to seek expertise continues to the present day, a revelation that was made especially noteworthy when the Kentucky Department of Corrections decided to up its dosage level of sodium pentathol. As Judge Crittenden explains, "[n]or were any medical personnel consulted in 2004 when the lethal injection protocol dosage of sodium thiopental . . . was increased from 2 grams to 3 grams." . . .

I did think Judge Crittenden's decision rang of naiveté in some places. He seemed to put more medical trust than is warranted in the Department of Corrections personnel, despite his recognition of their lack of qualifications. . . .

Likewise, Judge Crittenden acknowledges that sodium thiopental and pancuronium bromide can precipitate and clog the tubes distributing the chemicals to the inmate's body and also that the Department of Corrections provides no device to monitor the level of an inmate's consciousness. Again, however, he states that the risks of these occurrences are minimal. I think he is wrong. Such seemingly minor indications of ignorance concerning the lethal injection procedure have been linked to major lethal injection botches in this country. I have confidence that another court will address these kinds of problems in the future.

Overall, however, Judge Crittenden provided an impressive opinion. I do think the holding would have been more consistent with the other points and clarifications Judge Crittenden makes had he declared lethal injection unconstitutional. Regardless, Judge Crittenden's decision is a far bolder declaration than the press seems to have realized and its conclusions make great progress in the direction of reforming the lethal injection procedure.

Putting Juvenile Murderers to Death Is Wrong

Craig M. Bradley

Craig M. Bradley is a professor of law at the Indiana University School of Law in Bloomington.

In *Roper v. Simmons*, the Supreme Court reversed a 1989 precedent and struck down the death penalty for crimes committed by people under age 18. Although the Court's claim that standards of decency have evolved significantly in that period is less than compelling, the result seems right.

The majority reached its conclusion in the face of a heinous murder, but that is probably because it takes a particularly compelling case for a jury to sentence a juvenile to death. When Christopher Simmons was 17, he started talking about wanting to murder someone. On several occasions he discussed a plan—to commit a burglary, then tie up the victim and push him or her from a bridge—with his friends. He said they could "get away with it" because they were minors.

The Murder of Shirley Crook

Following this plan, he and a younger friend broke into the home of Shirley Crook. They bound and blindfolded her with duct tape and drove her to a state park. There they walked her to a railroad trestle, tied her hands and feet with electrical wire, covered her whole face with duct tape, and threw her into the river, where she drowned.

Because Simmons later bragged about the murder, the crime was not difficult to solve. Once in custody, he confessed

Craig M. Bradley, "The Right Decision on the Juvenile Death Penalty," *TRIAL*, vol. 41, no. 6, June 2005, pp. 60–62. Reprinted with permission of *TRIAL* (June 2005). Copyright American Association for Justice, formerly Association of Trial Lawyers of America.

and performed a videotaped reenactment of the crime. As a consequence, the guilt phase of the trial in Missouri state court was uncontested.

At the penalty phase, both sides brought up Simmons's age—the defense attorney arguing that he should not receive an adult sentence (meaning death) because he was not old enough to drink, serve on juries, or even see certain movies, and the prosecutor suggesting that his youthfulness made him all the more "scary."

The Court noted that . . . 30 [states] currently prohibit juvenile executions.

After Simmons's conviction was affirmed on appeal, the U.S. Supreme Court held in *Atkins v. Virginia* that the Eighth Amendment's prohibition of cruel and unusual punishment proscribes execution of the mentally retarded because "mental retardation . . . diminishes personal culpability even if the offender can distinguish right from wrong."

Eighth Amendment Prohibits Execution of Juveniles

Simmons then petitioned for post-conviction relief, and Missouri's high court reversed his death sentence, concluding that *Atkins* suggested that the Eighth Amendment also prohibited the execution of juveniles.

The U.S. Supreme Court, in the opinion by Justice Anthony Kennedy, began its analysis by saying it has long held that "evolving standards of decency" govern the prohibition of cruel and unusual punishment. The Court recognized that in 1989, in *Stanford v. Kentucky*, it had upheld the death penalty for 16- and 17-year-olds after having struck it down the previous year for those under 16.

But the Court also upheld the death penalty for the retarded in 1989 and then reversed that decision in *Atkins*. The question became whether—either because of statistics or a similarity in the moral issues involved in executing retarded and juvenile offenders—*Stanford* should also be reversed.

Beginning with the statistics, the Court noted that the same number of states—30—currently prohibit juvenile executions as had prohibited mentally disabled executions before *Atkins*. This includes the 12 states that prohibit the death penalty altogether. Moreover, only three states had actually executed a juvenile in the last 10 years.

Lies, Damned Lies, and Statistics

But in an illustration of former British Prime Minister Benjamin Disraeli's maxim that there are "lies, damned lies, and statistics," the dissenters pointed out that there were "currently over 70 juvenile offenders on death row in 12 different states (13 including the respondent)" and that the 18 death penalty states that forbid execution of juveniles constitute only 47 percent of states that allow the death penalty. "Words have no meaning if the views of less than 50 percent of the death penalty states can constitute a national consensus," Justice Antonin Scalia averred.

There is a scientific consensus that teenagers have 'an underdeveloped sense of responsibility.'

Still, the fact that only three states have actually executed juveniles in the last 10 years does suggest that there is very limited enthusiasm for this punishment.

Teenagers Have an Underdeveloped Sense of Responsibility

The majority was on stronger ground in noting that "capital punishment must be limited to those offenders who commit a narrow category of the most serious crimes and whose extreme culpability makes them the most deserving of execution." Since there is a scientific consensus that teenagers have "an underdeveloped sense of responsibility," it is unreasonable to classify them among the most culpable offenders: "From a moral standpoint, it would be misguided to equate the failings of a minor with those of an adult, for a greater possibility exists that a minor's character deficiencies will be reformed."

The Court tellingly recognized that this moral position was supported by the American Psychiatric Association, which forbids diagnosing any patient under 18 as a psychopath or a sociopath because psychiatrists can't distinguish between juveniles "whose crime reflects unfortunate yet transient immaturity and the rare juvenile offender whose crime reflects irreparable corruption." If psychiatrists can't make that distinction, then it is too much to ask jurors to do it.

Finally, the Court pointed out that only seven countries in the world have executed juveniles since 1990: Iran, Pakistan, Saudi Arabia, Yemen, Nigeria, the Democratic Republic of Congo, and China. Yet even these countries now disallow the juvenile death penalty, leaving the United States the only country to still permit it.

Justice John Paul Stevens, joined by Justice Ruth Bader Ginsburg, noted in a brief concurrence that if death penalty standards had not evolved since the drafting of the Eighth Amendment, it would still be permissible to execute seven-year-olds.

Dissenting, Justice Sandra Day O'Connor agreed that death penalty jurisprudence must depend on evolving standards of decency and that these would include developments in foreign law. However, she said, while immaturity should be taken into account in assessing whether to sentence a juvenile to death, execution should still be an option for the jury in particularly heinous cases. She argued that *Atkins* does not govern this case because, whereas the retarded are by definition deficient in their cognitive and moral capabilities, juveniles merely tend to be. Accordingly, it should be up to the jury to make that assessment in each case.

Dissent on the Court

In contrast, Scalia, joined by Chief Justice William Rehnquist and Justice Clarence Thomas, heaped scorn on every aspect of the majority opinion:

> The Court . . . proclaims itself sole arbiter of our nation's moral standards—and in the course of discharging that awesome responsibility purports to take guidance from the views of foreign courts and legislatures. Because I do not believe the meaning of our Eighth Amendment, any more than the meaning of other provisions of our Constitution, should be determined by the subjective views of five members of this Court and like-minded foreigners, I dissent.

As noted, Scalia's point about statistics—that those used by the Court to show that a "consensus" had developed among the states to oppose the juvenile death penalty were less than overwhelming—is well taken. He was on weaker ground in rejecting the majority's point that juveniles are considered legally irresponsible in a number of ways, such as voting, serving on juries, and marrying without parental consent. Citing *Stanford*, he said that a 16-year-old is mature enough to "understand that murdering another human is profoundly wrong."

But the majority would agree with this, and that's why life imprisonment of juveniles for murder is allowed. The question is not even whether an individual juvenile might have the level of moral culpability to be eligible for the death penalty. Rather, as the majority makes clear, the issue is whether we should allow juries, influenced by the facts of a heinous crime, to make that determination when professional psychiatrists are unable to do so.

Impact of Foreign Laws

Scalia also disagreed with the majority's reference to foreign sources, arguing that these are irrelevant to the meaning of our Constitution. Foreign laws are often either more liberal or more conservative than ours, he said, but so what?

Ironically, one example he used to make this point is that courts in other countries do not automatically exclude evidence in criminal cases when it is obtained unlawfully. He cited former Chief Justice Warren Burger's dissent in the 1971 case *Bivens v. Six Unknown Federal Narcotics Agents*, arguing that the exclusionary rule was "unique to American jurisprudence." This argument was later echoed by then Associate Justice Rehnquist in a 1979 opinion. Rehnquist joined Scalia's opinion in *Simmons*. Yet the point that Burger and Rehnquist were making in those earlier cases was that foreign law is useful in determining what our constitutional rules should be—as long as foreign law supports your position. So even if Scalia himself would never look to foreign sources to help understand our Constitution, his fellow conservatives have not hesitated to do so when it suits them.

The willingness of a substantial minority of state legislatures to allow the ultimate penalty for killers as ruthless and cold-blooded as Simmons is understandable. But the impossibility of making rational distinctions between those juveniles whose culpability is limited by their youth and those who are beyond reform justifies the conclusion of both the Supreme Court and foreign countries that execution of juvenile offenders should not be permitted.

Physicians Have an Ethical Responsibility Not to Participate in Executions

Peter A. Clark

Peter A. Clark is an associate professor of theology and health administration at Saint Joseph's University in Philadelphia.

To circumvent objections that the death penalty was "cruel and unusual punishment" and therefore a violation of the Eighth Amendment to the Constitution, advocates proposed lethal injection and the involvement of physicians to overcome the negative perceptions associated with the death penalty, and to increase public acceptability of the practice. Initiated in 1982, lethal injection is now the primary method of execution in 37 of the 38 states with the death penalty. "To be exact, this method has been used to kill 788 of the 956 men and women who have been executed in the United States since 1976, when the death penalty was reinstated by the Supreme Court." More recently, of the 191 executions performed in the United States since 2001, 189 have been by lethal injection.

This "medicalization" of the death penalty has ignited a debate, by those within the medical profession and by others outside it, about the appropriateness of physicians participating in executions. "This image of a white-coated symbol of care working with or as the black-hooded executioner is in striking contrast to established physician ethics, which bar physicians from involvement with executions." Physicians participating as "agents" of the State in state-sponsored executions argue that their presence ensures a more humane execution. They are being compassionate and caring by not

Peter A. Clark, "Physician Participation in Executions: Care Giver or Executioner?" *Journal of Law, Medicine & Ethics*, Spring 2006, pp. 95–98, 102–103. Reproduced by permission.

abandoning their patient at his/her time of need and by making sure the prisoner does not experience unnecessary pain or suffering. Some proponents even argue that this whole debate is nothing more than a ruse by death penalty abolitionists to end capital punishment in the United States. Opponents argue physician participation violates the Hippocratic Oath which clearly states that physicians should never do harm to anyone. The goal may appear to be to reduce pain and suffering, but in reality the physician's participation only maximizes efficiency. Opponents further argue that there is a profound conflict of purpose, role or interest. Despite objections by the American Medical Association (AMA) and other medical societies, a study of physicians' attitudes about participation in executions by Neil Farber, et al., found that the majority of physicians surveyed approved of most disallowed actions involving capital punishment, indicating that they believed it is acceptable in some circumstances for physicians to kill individuals against their wishes. This debate pits one ethical principle—beneficence—against another, nonmaleficence. The basic question is whether medicine has a role in addressing more competent and compassionate ways of executing people. . . .

Overview of Physician Participation in Executions

The death penalty is as old as recorded history, but most people are unaware that physicians' participation in it also has a long history. The earliest recorded physicians' involvement in the death penalty dates back to 1789 when French physicians—and notable opponents of the death penalty—Antoine Louis and Joseph-Ignace Guillotin developed a device to behead the condemned, which they believed was far more humane and civilized than methods of that day. The "guillotine" or "louisette" was used in France from 1792 to 1877 before capital punishment was abolished in 1881. It should be noted that Dr. Guillotin became shocked and disillusioned by the impact of his efforts, which facilitated capital punishment, and made his name a symbol of killing. For nearly two centuries the medical role in executions was driven by a desire to lessen the suffering of the condemned (and thus of the witnesses), or by a more mundane willingness to play the part insisted on by the state—to assist in bureaucratic aspects of transforming a prisoner to a corpse and to certify death. However, medical expertise is not a requirement to find or use a method of killing that minimizes suffering. Humane methods of killing animals have been utilized since before modern medicine. While Dr. Guillotin may have based his method on medical knowledge, a similar method of using a razor-sharp knife to sever the soft tissue of the neck had already existed for thousands of years.

Lethal injection subsequently became the method of choice by states not only because of its low cost, but also because it was viewed as being more humane.

In 1887, a commission of American physicians lobbied for the method of electrocution as a more humane alternative to hanging, claiming that hanging was imprecise, undignified, and unnecessarily unpleasant for criminals. New York State established its committee, chaired by a dentist, to investigate alternative methods of execution. Following the recommendations of the committee, New York constructed an electric chair which, as Thomas Edison testified, would lead to instantaneous death and was therefore considered more humane. It is documented that two American physicians, Dr. Carlos MacDonald and Dr. E. C. Spitzka, supervised the first use of the electric chair as a method of execution.

Oklahoma Begins Lethal Injections

A more recent attempt to make executions more humane and less painful was in the mid-1970s, when Oklahoma's electric chair needed to be replaced, which was likely to be expensive. A professor of anesthesiology in Oklahoma responded to a request from the state to develop a cheap and effective chemical form of execution. He created a three drug "cocktail" that included a fast-acting anesthetic, a muscle-paralyzing agent, and a cardio-toxin. To administer lethal injection, the condemned person is typically strapped to a chair or a trolley. Two intravenous lines are inserted, one is a backup. The lines are kept open with saline solution. At the warden's signal, the injection team administers the three drug "cocktail." The first person to be executed by this method was Charlie Brooks, in Texas in 1982. He died under the combined effect of sodium thiopental, pancuronium bromide, and potassium chloride. Two physicians were present for the execution and were heard to advise the executioner during the procedure.

Physician involvement not only violates . . . the Hippocratic Oath that is over two thousand years old, but violates the more recent Code of Medical Ethics.

Lethal injection subsequently became the method of choice by states not only because of its low cost, but also because it was viewed as being more humane. Although the electric chair was originally introduced for the same reasons, a number of cases involved torturous suffering. This began a movement to make electrocution unconstitutional under the cruel and unusual punishment clause of the Eighth Amendment. The use of lethal injection not only overcame the objections of cruel and unusual punishment, but incorporated a standard medical procedure as its foundation. Lethal injection by intravenous catheter can be indistinguishable from the intravenous infusion of any therapeutic solution commonly used in hospitals for antibiotics, electrolytes, or re-hydrating fluids. The process of medically inserting the catheter is the same. The only difference in a lethal injection is the identity and desired effect of the fluids actually infused.

The "medicalization" of lethal injection and thus the increased public acceptability of it have been further advanced by at least 28 states requiring the presence of a physician at the execution, and another five states which claim a physician "may" be present. According to *Human Rights Watch*:

> since these laws do not indicate the purpose of the physician's presence, one can only surmise that medical expertise is desired by the state to ensure that the procedure runs smoothly, in case something goes awry, or to pronounce death. Mere physician "presence" in the execution chamber risks conveying the message that the execution is countenanced by the medical profession.

Violation of Code of Medical Ethics

In a study of executions in the state of Illinois in the 1990s by Howard Wolinsky, physician involvement in lethal injections included setting up of intravenous portals for delivery of the execution drugs, monitoring vital signs, and pronouncing death. During a double execution, the physicians in question are reported to have even administered the intravenous drugs. However, no one knows this for certain because a state law passed in 1991 allows anonymity of the physicians involved in assisting lethal injection, and orders that they be paid in untraceable cash. Physician involvement not only violates a basic tenet of the Hippocratic Oath that is over two thousand years old, but violates the more recent *Code of Medical Ethics* by the American Medical Association.

Opposition to physician involvement in executions can be traced back to the Hippocratic Oath, which states: "I will prescribe regimen for the good of my patients according to my ability and my judgment and never do harm to anyone. To please no one will I prescribe a deadly drug, nor give advice which may cause his death." The Oath broadly condemns any physician whose action has the intent of causing harm or death. In more recent times, even though the AMA does not take a stand on the issue of capital punishment itself, it is quite clear that physicians should not be part of the process. In 1980, the Council of Ethical and Judicial Affairs of the AMA stated that, "physician participation in executions contradicts the dictates of the medical profession by causing harm rather than alleviating pain and suffering." This position was expanded and reaffirmed in 1992 and 1997. The Council's report was used as the basis for Current Opinion 2.06 of the AMA's *Code of Medical Ethics*. It states:

> An individual's opinion on capital punishment is the personal moral decision of the individual. A physician, as a member of a profession dedicated to preserving life when there is hope of doing so, should not be a participant in a legally authorized execution. Physician participation in an execution is defined generally as actions which would fall into one or more of the following categories: (1) an action which would directly cause the death of the condemned; (2) an action which would assist, supervise, or contribute to the ability of another individual to directly cause the death of the condemned; (3) an action which could automatically cause an execution to be carried out on the condemned prisoner.

The AMA's *Code of Medical Ethics* spells out what physician participation in an execution includes. The following actions are included:

> Prescribing or administering tranquilizers and other psychotropic agents and medications that are part of the execution procedure; monitoring vital signs on site or remotely (including monitoring electrocardiograms); attending or observing an execution as a physician; and rendering technical advice regarding execution.

In particular cases when the method of execution is lethal injection, the AMA stipulates the following actions as constituting physician participation in execution:

Selecting injection sites; starting intravenous lines as a port for a lethal injection device; prescribing, preparing, administering, or supervising injection drugs or their doses or types; inspecting, testing, or maintaining lethal injection devices; and consulting with or supervising lethal injection personnel.

Obtaining accurate information about the number of physicians who participate in executions is difficult because states generally refuse to name anyone who does so, citing security and privacy concerns.

The AMA recognizes that someone should oversee the technical aspects of the execution to reduce pain and suffering, but argues that "even when the method of execution is lethal injection, the specific procedures can be performed by nonphysicians with no more pain or discomfort for the prisoner."

Physician Secret Involvement in Executions

In March of 1994, the AMA and other groups called for licensing boards to consider physician complicity in capital sentences to be grounds for disciplinary proceedings, including revocation of licensure. However, in 2002, Dr. Jonathan Groner, surgery professor at Ohio State University, stated that "the AMA has never sanctioned anybody who participates in executions." It is estimated that about 28 states allow or require physicians to be present at executions. But obtaining accurate information about the number of physicians who participate in executions is difficult because states generally refuse to name anyone who does so, citing security and privacy concerns. At least eight states, including Georgia, also seek to shield physicians from professional discipline through laws stating that aiding in executions is not the practice of medicine. The issue hinges on whether this is a medical procedure or not. [Physician Kenneth] Baum argues that:

Other than these legislative decrees, what is it about such actions that remove them from the practice of medicine? Under any other circumstance, we view these same behaviors as the practice of medicine: selecting drugs, inserting catheters, monitoring vital signs, and pronouncing death. If this is not the practice of medicine, then much of what physicians do, such as prescribing medications and providing immunizations, is likewise not the practice of medicine.

This issue came to the public's attention with the case of Dr. Sanjeeva Rao, who is the attending physician at the state prison in Jackson, Georgia. When the state of Georgia started lethal injections in 2000, Dr. Rao started taking an active role in the executions. While he does not administer the injection, he does monitor the process. However, in 2001 Dr. Rao inserted a catheter into a prisoner's right subclavian vein after a nurse had tried unsuccessfully for 39 minutes to find a suitable vein in the prisoner's right arm, hand, leg and foot. This action led Dr. Arthur Zitrin, retired professor of Psychiatry at New York University and self-described death penalty abolitionist, to attempt to have Dr. Rao expelled from the American College of Physicians (ACP) for violating the AMA's *Code of Medical Ethics*. The effort failed when the ACP, an internists' organization, determined that Dr. Rao was behind in his dues and thus no longer a member. Dr. Zitrin subsequently filed a complaint against Dr. Rao with the Georgia Composite State Board of Medical Examiners seeking an investigation and appropriate sanctions against Dr. Rao for his participation in executions. Dr. Zitrin has also filed similar complaints against physicians in Illinois and Virginia. The problem is that the states appear to have contradictory laws. On the one hand, a physician can be disciplined by state medical boards for violating codes of medical ethics. On the other hand, numerous states allow and require physicians to be present at executions and protect their identity because the law states that aiding in executions is not actually the practice of medicine.

The American College of Physicians, *Human Rights Watch*, the National Coalition to Abolish the Death Penalty, and Physicians for Human Rights have joined forces to influence the position of the State Medical Societies on the question of physician participation in executions. They are insisting that each medical society have a written policy opposing medical participation in executions, support physicians who refuse to participate, and impose sanctions on those who do. Their hope is that with a concerted effort by physicians to protest medical participation in executions, capital punishment will grind to a halt in those states that require the presence of a physician—at least until the legislatures reformulate the existing laws and regulations.

Almost half [of surveyed physicians] said there was nothing wrong with physicians actually injecting condemned inmates with lethal drugs.

Many Physicians Believe Participation Is Ethical

This may be an uphill battle. In a survey published by Dr. Neil Farber and colleagues in the *Archives of Internal Medicine* in 2000, an overwhelming majority of physicians (74%) said it is acceptable for physicians to pronounce an executed inmate dead. Almost half the respondents—43%—said there was nothing wrong with physicians actually injecting condemned inmates with lethal drugs. Only 3% of the respondents were even aware that the AMA had published any ethical guidelines on this issue. Given these findings, it is not surprising that physicians willingly participate in executions and many of them believe it is even ethical to do so because of a sense of citizen obligation. The ethical confusion centers on the role of a physician to minimize pain and suffering which is consistent with the principle of beneficence, versus the direct causing of harm, which is consistent with the principle of non-maleficence. . . .

A physician's opinion on capital punishment is the personal opinion of that individual. However, as a physician he or she has the ethical responsibility to abide by the *Code of Medical Ethics* that governs the actions of those in the medical profession. The AMA's position on physician participation in executions, which embodies the spirit of the Hippocratic Oath, is quite clear that "a physician, as a member of a profession dedicated to preserving life when there is hope of doing so, should not be a participant in a legally authorized execution." The AMA sees its role in protecting values and services that may otherwise be vulnerable in society because of overshadowing by government, as is the case for executions, or by the private sector. Despite the fact that physician participation in executions violates the basic tenet of the Hippocratic Oath and the position of the AMA, not to mention similar positions of other medical societies, physicians continue to participate. . . .

Physicians' personal and societal values seem to trump their professional values. However, these arguments fall apart when examined and scrutinized from an ethical perspective.

They [physicians] are being used by certain states to medicalize executions in order to make them more palatable to the American public and to prevent capital punishment from being declared unconstitutional.

Some have argued that the way to circumvent the dilemma of physician participation is to train other medical personnel, such as physician assistants, nurses, etc., to perform the same task as the physician. This argument is clearly illogical. It assumes that other health care professionals are less dedicated to the ethical ideals of the medical profession. One might assume that all health care professionals are bound by the same basic ethical standards such as never intentionally harming anyone. In fact, the current professional oaths and position statements of both the American Nursing Association and the American Academy of Physician Assistants prohibit member participation in executions on ethical grounds. Logic and consistency would dictate that all medical professionals are bound by the same ethical arguments and constraints. Other physicians have tried to argue that their participation in executions is beneficent because it minimizes the risk of a botched procedure and thus minimizes pain and suffering. However, it has been shown that lethal injection, while on the surface may appear to be a painless way to die, in reality may be far more cruel and painful than anyone originally imagined. How any physician, who is dedicated to "preserving life when there is hope," can argue that taking the life of a healthy person because the state commands it is in the patient's best interest and does not conflict with the goals of medicine is beyond comprehension. Physician participation in executions is unethical because it violates the four basic principles that govern medical ethics: respect for persons, beneficence, nonmaleficence, and justice.

Physicians Are Being Exploited by States

The fear of many is that some physicians have been co-opted by the penal authorities and state legislatures in this country to believe that physician participation is a civic duty and one that is in the prisoner's best interest. In reality, these physicians are being used as a means to an end. They are being used by certain states to medicalize executions in order to make them more palatable to the American public and to prevent capital punishment from being declared unconstitutional because it is "cruel and unusual punishment." A basic tenet of the principle of respect for persons is that one may never use another person as a means to an end. Legislating that physicians must be present at executions uses these physicians as pawns, or means, in order to legitimize capital punishment. This not only violates the rights of these physicians but violates the basic ethical principles of the medical profession and distorts the physicians' role in society. The AMA and other medical societies should take a strong position that participation of physicians in executions is grounds for revoking a physician's license. "Even though state legislatures may attempt to subvert this position by guaranteeing anonymity to physicians who serve as executioners, the risk of losing one's license should serve as a deterrent." Until the AMA and other medical societies back up their positions with concrete actions, the image of a "white-coated healer" will continue to be confused with that of the "black-hooded executioner." This does not bode well for the medical profession or society as a whole, "because when the healing hand becomes the hand inflicting the wound, the world is turned inside out."

Current
CONTROVERSIES

CHAPTER 2

Is Capital Punishment Administered Fairly?

Chapter Preface

Today even some longtime supporters of the death penalty have concerns that capital punishment may not be administered fairly in all cases. The state of Illinois, for example, is in the seventh year of its moratorium on the death penalty. In 2000, Governor George Ryan of Illinois, once an avid supporter of capital punishment, declared the moratorium because of the state's dismal track record of exonerating more death row inmates than it executed. Since the state reinstated the death penalty in 1977, Illinois exonerated thirteen death row inmates and put to death twelve others. The issue garnered massive public attention across the country when Anthony Porter, an African American gang member living in Chicago, was released from prison for a crime he did not commit. Porter had spent fifteen years on death row and was within fifty hours of being executed. Porter's family was so certain of his impending death that they had planned his funeral arrangements.

The circumstances surrounding Porter's arrest and subsequent trial were so egregious that they cast doubt on the convictions of other death row inmates in Illinois and across the United States. Porter had been convicted of two murders. Both victims were shot to death in the bleachers overlooking a swimming pool on the South Side of Chicago on a late summer night in 1982. The so-called eyewitness first told investigators that he had not seen the shooter. After seventeen hours of police interrogation, the man changed his story, claiming that he had actually seen Porter shoot the man and the woman. At the time, police ignored information that a man named Alstroy Simon had recently had a dispute with one of the victims over drug money. Simon, who moved to Milwaukee soon after the murders, was not considered a prime suspect. Despite the lack of physical evidence connecting Porter to the horrible crimes, he was arrested and charged with double murder. The jury found him guilty after only nine hours of deliberations.

Porter was not only a victim of a botched police investigation, but he also received unethical and inferior legal representation. The presiding judge's conduct was also highly suspect. Porter's family retained a private attorney, who stopped investigating the case when the family could not pay the agreed-upon legal fee. At the trial, the same attorney once fell asleep, and the judge had to wake him. Further, the judge failed to sufficiently consider a defense motion for mistrial after it was learned that a juror attended the same church as one of the victims. After an investigation lasting several seconds, the judge denied the motion and sentenced Porter to death.

Less than two days before Porter was scheduled to die, the Illinois Supreme Court granted a stay of execution, ordering the lower court to determine whether the defendant was mentally fit to be executed. Porter tested so low on an IQ test that the court was not sure he could comprehend that he was about to be executed and why. His new attorneys sought the investigative assistance of Northwestern University's Center for Wrongful Convictions, located in Evanston, Illinois, and the university's Medill School of Journalism. The investigators obtained evidence of Porter's innocence when Alstroy Simon confessed to them on videotape. Porter was released from prison: Simon pleaded guilty of two counts of second-degree murder and was sentenced to thirty-seven and a half years in prison. Porter became the tenth person to be found innocent after being sentenced to death in Illinois.

The Chance of Executing an Innocent Person Is Very Slight

Richard A. Posner

Richard A. Posner is a judge of the U.S. Court of Appeals for the Seventh Circuit and a cofounder of American Law and Economics Review.

The recent execution by the State of California of the multiple murderer Stanley "Tookie" Williams has brought renewed controversy to the practice of capital punishment, a practice which has been abolished in about a third of the states and in most of the nations that the United States considers its peers; the European Union will not admit to membership a nation that retains capital punishment.

From an economic standpoint, the principal considerations in evaluating the issue of retaining capital punishment are the incremental deterrent effect of executing murderers, the rate of false positives (that is, execution of the innocent), the cost of capital punishment relative to life imprisonment without parole (the usual alternative nowadays), the utility that retributivists and the friends and family members of the murderer's victim (or in Williams's case victims) derive from execution, and the disutility that fervent opponents of capital punishment, along with relatives and friends of the defendant, experience. The utility comparison seems a standoff, and I will ignore it, although the fact that almost two-thirds of the U.S. population supports the death penalty is some, albeit weak (because it does not measure intensity of preference), evidence bearing on the comparison.

Richard A. Posner, "The Economics of Capital Punishment," *The Becker-Posner Blog*, December 18, 2005. www.Becker-Posner-blog.com. Reproduced by permission of the author.

Economic Studies Show Capital Punishment Is a Deterrent

Early empirical analysis by [economist] Isaac Ehrlich found a substantial incremental deterrent effect of capital punishment, a finding that coincides with the common sense of the situation: it is exceedingly rare for a defendant who has a choice to prefer being executed to being imprisoned for life. Ehrlich's work was criticized by some economists, but more recent work by economists Hashem Dezhbakhsh, Paul Rubin, and Joanna Shepherd provides strong support for Ehrlich's thesis; these authors found, in a careful econometric analysis, that one execution deters 18 murders. Although this ratio may seem implausible given that the probability of being executed for committing a murder is less than 1 percent (most executions are in southern states—50 of the 59 in 2004—which that year had a total of almost 7,000 murders), the probability is misleading because only a subset of murderers are eligible for execution. Moreover, even a 1 percent or one-half of 1 percent probability of death is hardly trivial; most people would pay a substantial amount of money to eliminate such a probability.

Although it may seem heartless to say so, the concern with mistaken execution seems exaggerated.

As for the risk of executing an innocent person, this is exceedingly slight, especially when a distinction is made between legal and factual innocence. Some murderers are executed by mistake in the sense that they might have a good legal defense to being sentenced to death, such as having been prevented from offering evidence in mitigation of their crime, such as evidence of having grown up in terrible circumstances that made it difficult for them to resist the temptations of a life of crime. But they are not innocent of murder. The number of people who are executed for a murder they did not commit appears to be vanishingly small.

It is so small, however, in part because of the enormous protraction of capital litigation. The average amount of time that a defendant spends on death row before being executed is about 10 years. If the defendant is innocent, the error is highly likely to be discovered within that period. It would be different if execution followed the appeal of the defendant's sentence by a week. But the delay in execution not only reduces the deterrent effect of execution (though probably only slightly) but also makes capital punishment quite costly, since there is a substantial imprisonment cost on top of the heavy litigation costs of capital cases, with their endless rounds of appellate and postconviction proceedings.

Mistaken Executions Are Rare

Although it may seem heartless to say so, the concern with mistaken execution seems exaggerated. The number of people executed in all of 2004 was, as I noted, only 59. (The annual number has not exceeded 98 since 1951.) Suppose that were it not for the enormous delays in execution, the number would have been 60, and the additional person executed would have been factually innocent. The number of Americans who die each year in accidents exceeds 100,000; many of these deaths are more painful than death by lethal injection, though they are not as humiliating and usually they are not anticipated, which adds a particular dread to execution. Moreover, for what appears to be a psychological reason (the "availability heuristic"), the death of a single, identified person tends to have greater salience than the death of a much larger number of anonymous persons. As [the Soviet dictator Joseph] Stalin is reported to have quipped, a single death is a tragedy, a million deaths is a statistic.

Executions Should Be Sped Up

But that's psychology; there is an economic argument for speeding up the imposition of the death penalty on convicted murderers eligible for the penalty; the gain in deterrence and reduction in cost are likely to exceed the increase in the very slight probability of executing a factually innocent person. What is more, by allocating more resources to the litigation of capital cases, the error rate could be kept at its present very low level even though delay in execution was reduced.

If murderers know that by 'reforming' on death row they will have a good shot at clemency, the deterrent effect of the death penalty will be reduced.

However, even with the existing, excessive, delay, the recent evidence concerning the deterrent effect of capital punishment provides strong support for resisting the abolition movement.

A final consideration returns me to the case of "Tookie" Williams. The major argument made for clemency was that he had reformed in prison and, more important, had become an influential critic of the type of gang violence in which he had engaged. Should the argument have prevailed? On the one hand, if murderers know that by "reforming" on death row they will have a good shot at clemency, the deterrent effect of the death penalty will be reduced. On the other hand, the type of advocacy in which Williams engaged probably had some social value, and the more likely the advocacy is to earn clemency, the more such advocacy there will be; clemency is the currency in which such activities are compensated and therefore encouraged. Presumably grants of clemency on such a basis should be rare, since there probably are rapidly diminishing social returns to death-row advocacy, along with diminished deterrence as a result of fewer executions. For the more murderers under sentence of death there are who publicly denounce murder and other criminality, the less credibility the denunciations have.

Capital Punishment Is Administered Fairly

Joshua Marquis

Joshua Marquis is the district attorney of Clatsop County, Astoria, Oregon.

For decades in America, questions about the death penalty centered on philosophical and sometimes religious debate over the morality of the state-sanctioned execution of another human being. Public opinion ebbed and flowed with support for the death penalty, declining as civil rights abuses became a national concern in the 1960s and increasing along with a rapid rise in violent crime in the 1980s.

Modern-Day Abolitionists

Those who oppose capital punishment call themselves "abolitionists," clearly relishing the comparison to those who fought slavery in the 19th century. In the mid-1990s these abolitionists, funded by a cadre of wealthy supporters including George Soros and Roderick MacArthur, succeeded in changing the focus of the debate over the death penalty from the morality of executions to questions about the "fundamental fairness" or, in their minds, unfairness of the institution. The abolitionists were frustrated by polling that showed that virtually all groups of Americans supported capital punishment in some form in some cases.

Led by Richard Dieter of the neutral-sounding Death Penalty Information Center, opponents of capital punishment undertook a sweeping make-over of their campaign. In addition to painting America as a rogue state—a wolf among the peace-

Joshua Marquis, "The Myth of Innocence," *Journal of Criminal Law and Criminology*, vol. 95, no. 2, 2005, pp. 501–508, 517–521. Copyright © 2005 by Northwestern University School of Law. Reprinted by special permission of Northwestern University School of Law, *Journal of Criminal Law and Criminology*.

ful lambs of the European Union who had forsaken the death penalty—the latter-day abolitionists sought to convince America that, as carried out, the death penalty was inherently racist, that the unfortunates on death row received wretched and often incompetent defense counsel, and, most appalling, that a remarkable number of those sentenced to death were in fact innocent.

Dieter and his allies pointed to the fact that while African-Americans make up only slightly more than ten percent of the American population, they constitute more than forty percent of those on death row. In addition, they described some cases in which the appointed lawyers were nothing more than golfing pals with the judge making the appointment, that some of these lawyers had no previous experience with murder cases, and that in at least one case the lawyer appears to have slept through portions of the trial.

Abolitionists painted a picture of massive prosecution, funded by the endless resources of the government and pitted against threadbare public defenders either barely out of law school or, if experienced, pulled from the rubbish heap of the legal profession.

But most compelling of all the arguments that called capital punishment "fatally flawed" were the stories of men who had served years on death row, a few coming close to their scheduled execution only to be released because a court had determined that they were "exonerated." Television programs showed dramatic footage of Anthony Porter, freed from Illinois's death row, running into the arms of his savior, Northwestern University journalism professor David Protess. A handful of other stories of "innocents on death row" filled magazines, television programs, and symposia on college campuses across the country.

In the face of horrific crimes like the murder of more than 160 people by Timothy McVeigh, death penalty opponents sought to recruit new converts. By the time of the 2000 presidential campaign, they had succeeded in moving the debate to a point where supporters of capital punishment felt beleaguered and outgunned. A growing number of classic conservatives, from William F. Buckley to Pat Robertson, expressed their mistrust of capital punishment. The arguments succeeded in driving down public support for the death penalty from a high of almost 80% in the late 1980s to a low of around 65% in the year George W. Bush ran against Al Gore for president [2000].

Moratorium on the Death Penalty

Recognizing that the polls still showed majority support for the existence of the death penalty, abolitionists started advocating for a "moratorium," suggesting that short of abolition, a halt should be declared to executions while the issue was intensively studied. They found an unlikely ally in then-Governor George Ryan of Illinois.

Just before leaving office in 2003, [Governor] Ryan stunned many when he announced a sweeping clemency, using his executive powers to release 164 men from death row.

Ryan, a conservative Republican, had just two years earlier, in 1998, won election in part by underlining his support for capital punishment. But in 1999 the *Chicago Tribune* began running a hard-hitting series of lengthy articles, accusing Illinois prosecutors of serious misconduct and highlighting a number of cases in which men sentenced to death row had been released when appellate courts found serious errors in their trials or claims of misconduct by police or prosecutors. Although prosecutors and at least one state Supreme Court justice questioned Ryan's authority simply to halt the death penalty process, Ryan's action effectively prevented the execution of any of the 170 men on that state's death row.

Ryan became a folk hero. He was lauded on college campuses across the country, cited as a profile in political courage by foreign politicians, and was even nominated for the Nobel Peace prize. Just before leaving office in 2003, Ryan stunned many when he announced a sweeping clemency, using his executive powers to release 164 men from death row and granting outright pardons to four more.

Sensing a possible sea change in public sentiment, the abolitionists pushed for other states to follow Ryan's example. The moratorium became a leading campaign issue in the Maryland governor's race in 2002, following the outgoing governor's decision to place a moratorium on that state's use of the death penalty and commission a study to determine whether race plays a role in the application of the death penalty.

After these apparent victories, the tide started to turn, but not in the way the abolitionists expected. Governor Ryan was dogged by a federal investigation into bribery and corruption charges that drove his approval rating to less than twenty-five percent. His name became so toxic in Illinois politics that a Republican candidate for governor in 2004, whose last name was also Ryan but was no relation to the Governor, campaigned on first name. After securing indictments and convictions against his top aides and even his campaign committee, federal prosecutors indicted Ryan on charges of bribery, corruption, and racketeering.

In Maryland, Democratic gubernatorial candidate Kathleen Kennedy Townsend, who had pledged her continued support for the death penalty moratorium, suffered a defeat in the 2002 election in the wake of the Washington-area sniper shootings. And, finally, the murder of 3,000 people on September 11, 2001, reminded many Americans that some crimes merited the ultimate punishment.

Having largely abandoned the moral arguments against capital punishment, the modern abolition movement is now based on a trio of urban legends: (1) the death penalty is racist at its core; (2) those accused of capital murder get grossly inadequate representation; and (3) a remarkable number of people on death row are innocent.

The Death Penalty Is Not Racist

In the last ten years the violent crime rate in America, including the murder rate, has decreased dramatically. A series of recent studies by economists showed an undeniable correlation between the death penalty and deterrence.

One researcher who reported that pardons may have actually cost lives nonetheless added a postscript to the study, saying that despite the results of his study he personally believed that the death penalty remained biased against minorities.

How could the death penalty not be racially biased given the disproportionate number of African-Americans convicted of murder? A Cornell University study issued in March of 2004 by law professors John Blume and Theodore Eisenberg and statistician Martin Wells—all opponents of the death penalty—showed that the conventional wisdom about the South's so-called "death belt," where blacks are said to be much more likely to die than whites convicted of similar murders, simply does not hold up. In the words of the authors, "[t]he conventional wisdom about the death penalty is incorrect in some respects and misleading in others."

A white murderer sentenced to death [is] twice as likely to actually be executed than a black person sentenced to death.

Until the Cornell study, the abolitionists had relied largely on the studies of David Baldus for their accusations of racism. Baldus, an Iowa law professor, claimed that race was a key factor in the imposition of death sentences. The Cornell University study, however, drawn from statistics gathered by the U.S.

Department of Justice's Bureau of Justice Statistics, showed that while African-Americans were convicted of committing 51.5% of all murders, they comprised only 41.3% of death row's population. The study revealed that roughly ten percent of the murders were cross-racial and that in twenty-eight states, including Georgia, South Carolina and Tennessee, blacks were under-represented on death row. States like Texas, which had the greatest number of people on death row, actually had a lower per capita rate of imposing the death penalty than Nevada, Ohio, and Delaware.

The Cornell study thereby confirmed what many prosecutors had suspected: that a white murderer sentenced to death was twice as likely to actually be executed than a black person sentenced to death. It may be shockingly politically incorrect to say, but the fact is that the most horrific murders—serial killings, torture murders, and sex crimes against children—tend to be committed more frequently by white murderers than blacks.

Capital Murder Defendants Receive Adequate Representation

The next urban legend is that of the threadbare but plucky public defender fighting against all odds against a team of sleek, heavily-funded prosecutors with limitless resources. The reality in the 21st century is startlingly different. There is no doubt that before the landmark 1963 decision in *Gideon v. Wainwright*, appointed counsel was often inadequate. But the past few decades have seen the establishment of public defender systems that in many cases rival some of the best lawyers retained privately. The *Chicago Tribune*, while slamming the abilities of a number of individual defense counsel in Cook County capital cases in the 1980s, grudgingly admitted that the Cook County Public Defender's Office provided excellent representation for its indigent clients.

Many giant silk-stocking law firms in large cities across America not only provide pro-bono counsel in capital cases, but also offer partnerships to lawyers whose sole job is to promote indigent capital defense. In one recent case in Alabama, a Portland, Oregon law firm spent hundreds of thousands of dollars of lawyer time on a post-conviction appeal for a death row inmate. In Oregon, where I have both prosecuted and defended capital cases, it is common for attorneys to be paid hundreds of thousands of dollars by the state for their representation of indigent capital clients. And the funding is not limited to legal assistance. Expert witnesses for the defense often total tens of thousands of dollars each, resources far beyond the reach of individual district attorneys who prosecute the same cases.

To call someone 'innocent' when all they managed to do was wriggle through some procedural cracks in the justice system . . . impeaches the moral authority of those who claim that a person has been 'exonerated.'

As the elected prosecutor of what is considered a mid-sized county in Oregon, I have a set budget that rarely gives me more than $15,000 a year to cover the total expenses of expert witnesses for *all* of the hundreds of cases my office prosecutes each year. Yet in one recent murder trial, one witness in the mitigation phase admitted he had already billed the state indigent defense program for over $30,000. In a related case the investigators for the defense were paid over $100,000.

Words Matter

Finally, and perhaps most importantly, we come to discuss why it matters whether someone is "innocent," "exonerated," "acquitted," or merely let go. Words like "innocence" convey enormous moral authority and are intended to drive the public debate by appealing to a deep and universal revulsion at the idea that someone who is genuinely blameless could wrongly suffer for a crime in which he had no involvement. But in the practice of law, words matter enormously. To call someone "innocent" when all they managed to do was wriggle through some procedural cracks in the justice system cheapens the word and impeaches the moral authority of those who claim that a person has been "exonerated." . . .

The justice system is far from perfect and has made many mistakes, mostly in *favor* of the accused. Hundreds, if not thousands, have died or lost their livelihoods through embezzlement or rape because the American justice system failed to incarcerate people who were guilty by any definition.

The Innocent Are Rarely Executed

Since the death penalty was re-authorized in 1976 by the Supreme Court, there have been upwards of 500,000 murders. About 7,000 murderers were sentenced to death and about 3,700 remain on death row today. About nine hundred and fifty have been executed. Appellate courts at the state and federal levels have imposed what one justice called "super due process" for convicted capital murderers, overturning almost two-thirds of all death sentences, a rate far exceeding that in other cases. Virtually none have been overturned because of "actual innocence."

Some claim that a civilized society must be prepared to allow ten guilty men to walk free in order to spare one innocent. But the well-organized and even better-funded abolitionists cannot point to a single case of a demonstrably innocent person executed in the modern era of American capital punishment.

Instead, let's tally the *additional* victims of the freed: *Nine*, killed by Kenneth McDuff, who had been sentenced to die for child murder in Texas and then was freed on parole after the death penalty laws at the time were overturned. *One*, by Robert Massie of California, also sentenced to die and also paroled. Massie rewarded the man who gave him a job on parole by murdering him less than a year after getting out of prison. *One*, by Richard Marquette, in Oregon, sentenced to "life" (which until 1994 meant about eight years in Oregon) for abducting and then dismembering women. He did so well in a woman-free environment (prison) that he was released—only to abduct, kill and dismember women again. *Two*, by Carl Cletus Bowles, in Idaho, guilty of kidnapping nine people and the murder of a police officer. Bowles escaped during a conjugal visit with a girlfriend, only to abduct and murder an elderly couple.

The victims of these men didn't have "close calls" with death. They are dead. Murdered. Without saying goodbye to their loved ones. Without appeal to the state or the media or Hollywood or anyone's heartstrings.

Discouraged over polls that have consistently shown public support for capital punishment between sixty-five and eighty-five percent over the last quarter century, proponents of the death penalty have decided to tap into an understandable horror that people who are truly innocent of the murder of which they stand convicted are on death row. They are turning into doe-eyed innocents the few murderers who have slipped through one of the countless cracks in the law afforded to capital defendants. They want us to believe that any one of us could be snatched at any time from our daily freedoms and sentenced to die because of a false and coerced confession, police corruption, faulty eyewitness identification, botched forensics, prosecutorial misconduct, and shoddy and ill-paid defense counsel.

There are a handful of people who have spent time, in some cases many years, on death row, for crimes they genuinely did not commit. The number bandied about by the abolitionists is just past the 100 mark. But a closer examination using a more realistic definition of innocence—that is, had no involvement in the death, wasn't there, didn't do it—drops the number to thirty or even twenty-five: At a seminar in February of 2004 held by the Federal Bar Council of New York, U.S. District Court Judge Jed Rakoff, who made history in 2001 by ruling the death penalty unconstitutional, acknowledged that his research showed the number to be closer to thirty. The larger question is whether the problem of wrongful convictions in capital cases is an episodic or epidemic problem. . . .

The number of death sentences is, in fact, decreasing. Criminal sentences for crimes other than murder have become tougher, terms of imprisonment more certain, and perhaps more significantly, the rate of murder is down overall. Prosecutors and juries are properly and appropriately becoming even more discriminating about determining who should die for their crimes. It is a journey not taken lightly.

Death penalty opponents risk losing their credibility when they are reckless with the truth.

Likewise, casting the accused as true innocents caught up by a corrupt and uncaring system only discredits a movement that has legitimate moral arguments. Nothing excuses making the victims nameless and faceless, making martyrs out of murderers, and turning killers into victims. . . .

In a subject as emotionally charged as the death penalty these claims must be made precisely—by all sides. Intellectual honesty is a critical ingredient to a meaningful discussion of this important subject. Death penalty opponents risk losing their credibility when they are reckless with the truth.

Death Row Reforms May Lead to a Fairer Criminal Justice System

Jean M. Templeton

Jean M. Templeton is a Chicago attorney who served as the research director for the Illinois Governor's Commission on Capital Punishment.

Change in the criminal-justice system is a rare thing. Change in death-penalty policy is even more rare. Yet Illinois undertook a comprehensive reassessment of its death-penalty system recently, passing reforms that will have far-reaching impacts on how murder trials are handled in the state—and that could serve as a model for reform in the rest of the country.

Following the review, 11 men were released from death row, and the furor over the death penalty only escalated after the 1999 release of death-row inmate Anthony Porter. Porter had been convicted of a double murder, believed to be a holdup gone bad, in a Chicago park in 1982. A mere 50 hours before Porter's execution, his lawyers made a last-ditch attempt to save him by asserting new questions about his mental competence. His execution was stayed, and in the intervening months, journalism students working in cooperation with a private detective located another man who confessed to the murder. Porter was released.

The case, and the flood of media attention that accompanied it, was enough to raise doubts about the death-penalty system even among death-penalty supporters, including

George Ryan, then the Republican governor of Illinois. In early 2000, Ryan took the bold step of declaring a moratorium on executions in the state until a panel of experts, the Illinois Governor's Commission on Capital Punishment, could make recommendations about how the system might be improved. In 2002, after two years of intensive study, the blue-ribbon commission released a report making 85 recommendations for improving the state's capital-punishment system. Late last year, the Illinois Legislature adopted many of the recommended reforms, and current Governor Rod Blagojevich has pledged to continue the moratorium until the reforms' effectiveness can be assessed.

Unfortunately, as extensive investigation by psychologists has shown, eyewitness evidence may not be especially reliable.

While both prosecution and defense supported many of the commission's recommendations, there were two that proved controversial. The first required videotaping of police interrogations; the second involved changes in lineup procedures to make eyewitness identifications more reliable. Both recommendations were initially opposed by law enforcement, and it took determined advocacy by legislators before they were included in last year's reforms. Now that they are law, they may produce far-reaching effects on the investigation of homicides in the state.

Eyewitness Evidence Is Not Very Reliable

Because we often believe that our eyes don't deceive us, we tend to think that eyewitness accounts of a crime are the very best evidence of what actually occurred. Certainly juries often find it persuasive. Unfortunately, as extensive investigation by psychologists has shown, eyewitness evidence may not be especially reliable. The Illinois commission therefore recommended broad changes in the procedures for police lineups.

In a lineup, an eyewitness to or victim of a serious crime views a group of people or photos at the police station. The crime suspect is among the group, and the witness is asked whether he or she can identify anyone in the lineup. Generally speaking, the law requires that the other people in the lineup bear some resemblance to the suspect's description so that the suspect won't stand out. If the witness or victim identifies one of the group, a report is made of the identification.

Research shows, however, that witnesses often choose the person in the lineup who looks most like the person who committed the crime. In other words, they make a *relative judgment*. This process may produce a correct identification if the actual suspect is present. But if he or she is not, many people will simply select the person who most resembles him or her. This selection of the wrong person, what social scientists call a "false positive," can lead to the prosecution of an innocent person.

Eradicate False-Positive Identification

In an effort to eradicate false positives, Iowa psychologist Gary Wells and others have developed an alternative identification procedure called a "sequential lineup." In this procedure, the eyewitness looks at each person in the lineup separately, without observing the others in the group. The eyewitness then makes more of an *absolute judgment* about that person before observing other people or photos in the lineup. This process reduces the rate of mistaken identifications without substantively reducing the number of accurate identifications.

A majority of the Illinois commission recommended adopting sequential lineups. However, because existing methods had already met with court approval, some commission members had reservations about mandating a procedure radically different from that which was already in place. But one legislator with fairly conservative views on the death penalty argued persuasively for the change.

Representative Julie Hamos, a Democrat, represents a relatively liberal district along the north-shore suburbs of Chicago. Early in her legal career, she served as a policy adviser for the Cook County state's attorney's office, the largest prosecutor's office in Illinois. Chicago Mayor Richard Daley, a conservative law-and-order Democrat, was the state's attorney in those days. Hamos herself supported the death penalty for heinous crimes.

Elected to the legislature in 1998, Hamos represents a district that includes many opponents of the death penalty. Troubled by the number of men released from death row in Illinois and affected by activism among her constituents on the issue, she began to modify her own views. Hamos also came to realize the frailties inherent in eyewitness testimony after conversations with Wells.

In 2002, she introduced a bill to require the use of sequential lineups. Prospects for passage seemed dim. But when the "Report of the Governor's Commission on the Death Penalty" was released in April of that year with a similar recommendation, Hamos renewed her efforts, working quietly among the Democratic leadership to ensure that the lineup proposals were on the table.

The measure failed that year, but as the legislature began its journey toward death-penalty reform in 2003, Hamos persuaded the leadership to include it again. In response to law-enforcement concerns, the proposal was limited to development of a pilot program that would enable the procedures to be tested in several police districts in the state. When that legislation passed in November 2003, sequential lineups were part of the bargain. By July 1, 2004, the Illinois State Police was to have identified three pilot police departments, one of which must be the city of Chicago, in which sequential lineups and photo spreads will be tested. A report on the program's effectiveness will be filed with the Illinois General Assembly . . .

Videotaping Interrogations

Not every homicide case involves eyewitnesses, however, which often leaves police the task of interrogating a suspect in order to try to obtain a confession. A person's confession of murder is powerful evidence to prove guilt, and under the law it must have been made voluntarily. Where there is some dispute over whether the statement is voluntary, a defendant may seek to prevent the use of the statement as evidence against him or her.

Videotaping the process is important because academic studies suggest that there are circumstances under which people will confess falsely.

As the debate over the inadequacies of the Illinois death-penalty system evolved, there were those who charged that some death-row convictions were based on confessions that were not true or not voluntary. Final statements in which a defendant confessed had been videotaped in the Cook County state's attorney's office since 1999. While videotaping these confessions has proven useful to demonstrate what the suspect actually said, critics complained that the program failed to capture the questioning process itself, in which undue pressure may be put on suspects to agree with the police version of events. Reformers in Illinois, including the governor's commission, pushed for the videotaping of the entire interrogation process.

Videotaping the process is important because academic studies suggest that there are circumstances under which people will confess falsely. One group known to do so are the mentally retarded, who sometimes confess in order to please authority figures. In 2000, a young Chicago man named Corethian Bell was arrested for killing his mother. Bell, described as mentally ill and borderline retarded, gave a videotaped confession that he had, indeed, killed his mother. Subsequent DNA testing, however, suggested that another man might have been guilty of the crime, and Bell was released from jail and charges against him dropped—despite his confession.

Suspects Brutalized to Confess

More troubling are confessions coming from those who may have been unduly pressured or abused. In the late 1980s, complaints began to surface that a group of Chicago police officers, led by then–Chicago Police Commander Jon Burge, had brutalized suspects in order to obtain confessions. The allegations went beyond rough treatment during arrest to claims of systematic torture. Suspects alleged that they were beaten, shocked with electrical currents, and threatened with being shot in order to compel confessions. Although Burge denied the charges, he was fired in 1993 for physical brutality against a suspect. None of the police officers alleged to have been involved faced criminal charges. In 2002, almost 10 years later, a special prosecutor was appointed to look into the allegations. Media reports suggest that the number of possible cases of torture has now risen to more than 100. The special prosecutor's report is expected sometime this year [2004].

Proponents of videotaping interrogations point to these incidents to support their case. Videotaping the entire process, they say, would protect suspects from abuses and police officers from unfounded charges of brutality. Yet in Illinois, the proposal failed to gain wide acceptance among police departments. Officials said it would interfere with police work or that it would be too costly. Bills to implement some form of videotaping of interrogations were introduced in the Illinois Legislature in 1999, but they never got a hearing. The Illinois House revisited the issue in 2001, and it did pass provisions requiring videotaped interrogations, but the bill did not get a hearing in the Illinois Senate. It was not until control of the state Senate changed hands in the 2002 elections that a videotaping bill appeared headed for passage.

Credit for getting the videotaping bill into the final death-penalty package has been largely attributed to state Senator Barack Obama, a Democrat from Chicago. Obama is now [in 2004] running a strong race for the U.S. Senate, which, if successful, would make him the third African American senator since Reconstruction. Elected to the Illinois Legislature in 1996, he is considered an extremely effective legislator. Rather than accept law-enforcement opposition to the bill, he brought law-enforcement officials to the table for discussion, eventually persuading them to drop their opposition.

In departments where interrogations are videotaped and initial police resistance overcome, we have seen positive benefits, including a sharpening of police interview skills.

Illinois thus became the first state in the nation to pass legislation requiring the videotaping of interrogations. The legislation applies to what are called "custodial interrogations"—those occurring at a police station—in all homicide cases. The law works by preventing statements made by a suspect from being admitted in a court proceeding unless the statement was recorded electronically. Under limited circumstances, the prosecution may use unrecorded statements in court if they prove that the statement was voluntarily given and is reliable. The provisions represent a significant change from prior law, which permitted the prosecution to use a statement made by a defendant and put the burden on the defendant to prove that the statement was not given voluntarily. Under the new law, the burden shifts to the prosecution to prove that a statement made outside of an electronic recording process was made voluntarily and is reliable.

Provisions requiring electronic recording do not take effect until 2005 in order to allow time to develop procedures governing the recording. In the meantime, legislation was passed to establish several pilot programs throughout the state to record interrogations in murder cases. These programs will help police agencies develop procedures on how videotaping the interrogation process should occur and provide training for police officers in how to conduct videotaped interrogations.

Death Penalty Reform Will Reduce All Types of Wrongful Convictions

In Illinois, these innovative proposals—videotaping interrogations and sequential lineups—apply not only to death-penalty cases but to others as well. While officials were initially reluctant to embrace the proposals, their widespread use will ultimately lead to better documentation of evidence and reduce wrongful convictions of all types. In departments where interrogations are videotaped and initial police resistance overcome, we have seen positive benefits, including a sharpening of police interview skills. Over the long term, police will likely come to appreciate these more rigorous investigative techniques.

Improvements in the death-penalty system have gathered increased support among legislators and the public. The reforms in Illinois passed by a nearly unanimous vote of the legislature. And public-opinion polling in February of 2003 suggests a softening of public attitudes on the death penalty in Illinois, with the percentage of state residents who support the death penalty at 55 percent, which is well below national polling figures.

Illinois Commission Is the National Standard

Meanwhile, DNA testing continues to be carried out, leading to the release of innocent men and women—more persuasive proof that our criminal-justice system makes mistakes, which is key in promoting death-penalty reform. The recommendations produced by the governor's commission in Illinois have become a standard by which other states have begun to evaluate their own death-penalty systems. In California, for instance, scholars have recently undertaken a systematic comparison of that state's death-penalty process with the Illinois recommendations and have illuminated many weaknesses.

In North Carolina, advocates of a death-penalty moratorium, modeled on Illinois Governor Ryan's, have gained ground with policy-makers. The North Carolina Senate passed moratorium provisions last year [in 2003], and advocates are seeking approval in the North Carolina House. Public-opinion polling done by moratorium supporters indicates that 63 percent of those polled favor a moratorium on executions in the state pending a review of the death-penalty system. The North Carolina Academy of Trial Lawyers has released its own list of reforms that should be considered during such a moratorium, including a number of the same substantive reforms suggested in Illinois.

The discussion over reforming the death-penalty system, and the successful passage of so many reforms, has led to a broader evaluation of the criminal-justice system in Illinois and elsewhere. Greater scrutiny of death-penalty cases involving wrongful convictions is slowly leading observers to ask whether there are other miscarriages of justice we have yet to uncover in the rest of the criminal-justice system, where cases are given a far less rigorous review. Death-penalty reforms, then, may be a first step on the road to broader evaluation of the criminal-justice system itself.

Wrongful Convictions Involving Prisoners Are Too Common

C. Ronald Huff

C. Ronald Huff is dean of the School of Social Ecology and a professor in the Department of Criminology, Law, and Society at the University of California, Irvine.

The U.S. experience with the problem of wrongful conviction extends throughout the nation's history, as is true for other nations, such as Canada, and predates the formation of the United States as an independent nation. As residents of a British possession, American colonists were often subjected to secret accusations without the right to question their accusers and were generally denied the types of due process rights that U.S. citizens have taken for granted since the development of the Constitution and the Bill of Rights. And, while status differences were generally less important in the colonies than in England, the American colonies were certainly not egalitarian, and some regions (especially Virginia) were quite conscious of distinctions in socio-economic status. This fact, along with the inferior social status assigned to blacks, suggests that class and race discrimination influenced decisions regarding who was guilty and how they should be punished. Sadly, such discrimination continues to occur today, despite important social and legal reforms, and is evident in many cases of wrongful conviction in the United States.

This article is not the place to dwell on the colonial roots of wrongful conviction; rather, its aim is to discuss the contemporary American experience. As I have noted elsewhere,

C. Ronald Huff, "Wrongful Convictions: The American Experience," *Canadian Journal of Criminology and Criminal Justice*, January 2004, pp. 107–120. © 2004 CJCCJ/RCCJP. Reprinted by permission of University of Toronto Press Incorporated. www.utp journals.com.

scholars, jurists, journalists, and activists have documented and analysed cases of wrongful conviction since [Edwin M.] Borchard's pioneering work more than seven decades ago. For more than half a century, the documentation and analyses focused almost exclusively on individual cases, but beginning in the 1990s, and continuing today, a decided shift has occurred in scholarly research, as well as in media attention and public opinion. The public policy importance of wrongful conviction has recently grown in the United States. Citizens' and policy makers' increasing awareness of this issue has been closely linked to the highly publicized post-conviction DNA exonerations of individuals who served long prison sentences and to the increasing abolition of, or moratoria on, the use of the death penalty in the United States. Recent studies involving the possibility of error in capital cases have brought even further attention—and a sense of urgency—to this issue. [A] seminal study [in 1992] argued that at least 23 innocent persons have already been executed in the United States. In a more recent and highly publicized study examining thousands of capital sentences over a 23-year period (1973–1995), [the authors] found serious, reversible errors in almost 70% of cases. Although the great majority of those who are wrongly convicted in the United States do not face the death penalty, or even life in prison, such errors often result in many years of unwarranted punishment and serious damage to the lives of the wrongly convicted, while the actual offenders in those cases are free to commit additional crimes, thus compromising public safety.

Thousands of People Are Wrongfully Convicted Each Year

No systematic data on wrongful conviction are kept in the United States, and certainly it is not possible at this point to accurately estimate or compare the magnitude or frequency of this problem across jurisdictions. In fact, estimating the extent to which wrongful conviction occurs is a much greater challenge than estimating the true incidence rate of crime, since victimization surveys (including cross-national surveys) have greatly facilitated the latter task, allowing us to extrapolate between official crime reports and victimization data. No similar credible methodology has been developed to estimate the true extent of wrongful conviction, since many cases go undiscovered and since analogous surveys of prisoners, for example, would lack public credibility.

The great majority of extant research suggests that eyewitness identification error is the factor most often associated with wrongful convictions.

A colleague and I conducted a survey, utilizing an intentionally conservative sample dominated by prosecutors, judges, and law enforcement officials and a national sample of attorneys general. The total sample size was 353, and we received 229 responses (a 65% response rate). We asked our conservative sample to *estimate* what proportion of all felony convictions resulted in wrongful convictions. Based on the responses we received, we then estimated an error rate of 0.5%, and we decided to see what it would really mean if the U.S. criminal justice system is, indeed, 99.5% accurate and errs in only 0.5% of all felony cases. Based on Uniform Crime Report data for 2000, if we assume that the system is 99.5% accurate, we can estimate that about 7,500 persons arrested for index crimes are wrongly convicted each year in the United States. The United States has such a large base rate of arrests for serious crimes that even a small error rate will produce thousands of wrongful convictions each year. [Another study], furthermore, recently reported that as a result of DNA testing conducted in 18,000 criminal cases, more than 25% of *prime suspects* were excluded prior to trial. Since the great majority of criminal cases do not produce biological material to be tested, one can only speculate as to the error rate in those cases. These findings raise serious questions about the accuracy of the U.S. criminal justice system.

Why Do Wrongful Convictions Occur?

Research in the United States has consistently found that the principal factors contributing to wrongful conviction include eyewitness error; over-zealous law enforcement officers and prosecutors who engage in misconduct, including withholding evidence; false or coerced confessions and suggestive interrogations; perjury; misleading line-ups; the inappropriate use of informants or "snitches"; ineffective assistance of counsel; community pressure for a conviction; forensic science errors, incompetence, and fraud; and the "ratification of error" (the tendency to "rubber-stamp" decisions made at lower levels as cases move up through the system). Usually, more than one factor contributes to the error, and there are interaction effects among these factors. For example, police or prosecutorial over-zealousness might be combined with perjury, withholding of evidence, and the inappropriate use of jailhouse informants—all occurring in a case in which the defendant has inadequate assistance of counsel and is therefore unable to discover these errors. Let us consider some of these factors.

Eyewitness Identification

The great majority of extant research suggests that eyewitness identification error is the factor most often associated with wrongful convictions. In our survey, 79% of our respondents ranked witness error as the most frequent type of error resulting in wrongful conviction [Barry] Scheck et al. report that in 84% of the DNA exonerations that they examined the conviction rested, at least in part, on mistaken eyewitness identification. . . . And other scholars have written extensively about eyewitness perception, how it can be significantly affected by psychological, societal, cultural, and systemic factors, and how police line-ups should and should not be conducted to ensure fairness to suspects.

Police and Prosecutorial Misconduct

Of the post-conviction DNA exonerations reported by Scheck et al. 63% involved police and/or prosecutorial misconduct. The authors also reported finding, in examining 381 murder convictions that had been reversed due to police or prosecutorial misconduct, that *not once* was a prosecutor disbarred, even after knowingly allowing perjured testimony or deliberately concealing exculpatory evidence. Most of the time, in fact, they were not even disciplined. Similarly, a recent study by the Center for Public Integrity found that since 1970, individual judges and appellate court panels have cited prosecutorial misconduct as a factor when dismissing charges at trial, reversing convictions or reducing sentences in more than 2,000 cases. An analysis of these cases revealed the following types of misconduct:

- Courtroom misconduct (making inappropriate or inflammatory comments in the presence of the jury; introducing or attempting to introduce inadmissible, inappropriate or inflammatory evidence; mischaracterizing the evidence or the facts of the case to the court or jury; committing violations pertaining to the selection of the jury; or making improper closing arguments);

- Mishandling of physical evidence (hiding, destroying or tampering with evidence, case files or court records);

- Failing to disclose exculpatory evidence;

- Threatening, badgering or tampering with witnesses;

- Using false or misleading evidence;

- Harassing, displaying bias toward, or having a vendetta against the defendant or defendant's counsel (including *selective* or *vindictive prosecution*, which includes instances of denial of a speedy trial);

- Improper behavior during grand jury proceedings.

False Confessions

Another important factor in wrongful convictions is false and coerced confessions, which are often related to suggestive interrogations. Scheck et al. report that 15 of the first 62 post-conviction DNA exonerations in their database, or about one in four, involved false confessions.

Five of the first 13 Illinois death row inmates found to have been wrongly convicted were prosecuted using information obtained from jailhouse informants.

Some law enforcement units seem especially prone to unethical behaviour. These include "elite" units that tend to operate with more independence from the rest of the organization, such as elite narcotics enforcement and street gang units. In the ... highly publicized Los Angeles Police Department scandal, for example, an excerpt from one officer's testimony illustrates the problem:

> Well, sir, make no bones about it, what we did was wrong—planting evidence ... fabricating evidence, perjuring ourselves—but our mentality was us against them ... We knew that Rampart's crime rate, murder rate, was the highest in the city ... [l]ieutenants, captains, and everybody else would come to our roll calls and say this has to end and you guys are in charge of things. Do something about it. That's your responsibility ... And the mentality was, it was like a war, us against them ...

Widespread Use of "Snitches"

Another important contributing factor is the widespread and often unprincipled use of informants, or "snitches," by police, prosecutors, and corrections officers. Five of the first 13 Illinois death row inmates found to have been wrongly convicted were prosecuted using information obtained from jailhouse informants, and 21% of the DNA exoneration cases reported by Scheck et al. involved the use of "jailhouse snitches." Such informants, many of whom have been used repeatedly, are often willing to shape their stories to fit whatever is needed, in return, of course, for favourable considerations of various kinds (or, sometimes, simply because they do not like the defendant or the nature of the crime with which he has been charged—for example, violent crimes against children, such as molestation or rape). These unreliable informants have often played key roles in convicting defendants, including those in capital cases. Major investigations concerning the use of jailhouse informants have been conducted in both the United States and Canada in recent years, culminating in recommendations for reform.

Ineffective Counsel

Ineffective assistance of counsel has been a basis for appeal in the U.S. since the famous Scottsboro Boys case (*Powell v. Alabama*, 1932) [nine black teenagers were sentenced to death for the gang rape of two white girls], but such appeals are rarely successful, despite widespread acknowledgement by judges at both state and federal levels that many attorneys are inadequately prepared for trial work. Unfortunately, being inadequately represented by defence counsel is a widespread problem that is likely to worsen as a result of the inadequate budgets allocated for defence work. Ineffective assistance of counsel poses a special problem and challenges the assumptions of the adversarial system of justice. Even more threatening to our adversarial system's assumptions are the "guilty plea wholesalers" who make comfortable livings by pleading defendants guilty without investigating cases or even interviewing the defendants.

Forensic Labs

Recent important advances in forensic science offer tremendous opportunities to improve the accuracy of our criminal justice system. However, the technology is ahead of the quality control, training, and, in some cases, ethics of those who work in crime labs. On the positive side, [Barry] Scheck and [Peter] Neufeld's Innocence Project has relied on DNA analyses to exonerate many wrongly convicted persons. On the negative side, some "junk scientists" have mishandled, misinterpreted, and even intentionally distorted evidence, helping to secure the convictions of innocent defendants.

The adversarial system relies on the skill and resources of the prosecution and the defence, and in criminal cases, the former nearly always enjoys considerably more resources than the latter.

In my judgement, forensic labs where evidence in criminal cases is analysed should be accredited, independent scientific laboratories with their own line item budgets, and their analyses should be equally available to both the prosecution and the defence. Unfortunately, in the United States these labs are nearly always part of a law enforcement organization. This organizational locus often subjects them to organizational cultures that emphasize convicting defendants ("We arrest them and you help convict them") instead of emphasizing scientific objectivity.

Unequal Adversarial System

In my judgement, a major contextual factor in the production of wrongful convictions in the United States is the adversarial system in which the U.S. criminal justice process unfolds. The adversarial system relies on the skill and resources of the prosecution and the defence, and in criminal cases, the former nearly always enjoys considerably more resources than the latter. These advantages include human resources (investigators, staff, etc.) as well as budgetary resources. In all too many cases, the defence counsel relies heavily, if not entirely, on the police investigation, rather than conducting an independent investigation to establish the facts. This means that the police investigation must be both thorough and objective, which is not always the case because of organizational pressures to move on to the next case (time and caseload pressures) and to press for a conviction (public and political pressures).

While both the adversarial and the inquisitorial systems replace private vengeance with state authority, the adversarial system places much greater emphasis on *process* than on simple truth-finding. This is apparent in a number of wrongful conviction cases wherein the convicted defendants sought reversals of their verdicts on the grounds that they were factually innocent (and, in some cases, had new evidence that could potentially exonerate them), only to learn that since they claimed no *procedural* violations, their chances for success were remote at best. A humorous story is told to illustrate this point with respect to the British system of adversarial justice. A frustrated English judge, having just finished listening to conflicting witness accounts, turned to the barrister and asked, "Am I never to hear the truth?" The barrister's reply: "No, my lord, merely the evidence."

The U.S. criminal justice system's accuracy is essential to its perceived legitimacy.

Defenders of the adversarial system argue that it is superior to other systems because justice is better served when the two sides present vigorous cases and the trier of fact decides the outcome. This proposition, however, assumes that both sides will present vigorous arguments and will have conducted thorough investigations to determine the facts of the case. These assumptions are highly questionable, given the resource issues noted above. A further defence of the adversarial system is that, lacking this type of individual-level responsibility for representing the defendant, the inquisitorial system does not ensure a thorough investigation and presentation of the facts either. . . .

Improve Accuracy of the Justice System

The factors leading to wrongful conviction in the United States and Canada are quite comparable, as are the impacts of wrongful convictions, including the devastating effects on the wrongly convicted, the loss of public confidence in the justice system, and the threat to public safety that occurs when we allow the actual offenders to remain free while the wrongly convicted are incarcerated.

In 360 BC, Plato made the following observation in *The Republic*, perhaps the finest of his Socratic dialogues:

> Mankind censure injustice fearing that they may be the victim of it, and not because they shrink from committing it.

It seems that not much has changed. It is therefore imperative that we continue to develop a better understanding of the particular type of injustice known as wrongful conviction and reduce its occurrence, both to protect the innocent and to protect society from continued victimization by criminals who may remain free while innocent persons go to prison or, perhaps, to their deaths. . . . The U.S. criminal justice system's accuracy is essential to its perceived legitimacy, and systematic attention must be paid to the errors that are committed and how those errors might be reduced. The same applies, of course, to the Canadian criminal justice system, and it is incumbent upon us to continue our efforts to improve the accuracy of both systems of justice and to better compensate those who become the victims of wrongful conviction.

The Death Penalty Is Not Applied Equally to Both Sexes

Victor L. Streib

Victor L. Streib is a law professor at Ohio Northern University and an attorney specializing in violent crime and the death penalty.

Picture in your mind a condemned murderer being sentenced to death, eating a last meal, or trudging ever-so-reluctantly into the execution chamber. In your mind's eye, do you see this wretched creature as a woman? Most of us do not, given that over ninety-nine percent of the people executed in the United States are men. Female offenders, both girls and women, are so seldom found on our death rows that, once condemned, they may be ignored and forgotten.

Death Row Women and the Media

We are occasionally made aware of women put to death through media coverage of high profile executions. A recent case with front-page national coverage was that of Karla Faye Tucker, executed in Texas on February 3, 1998. Tucker caught the attention of the popular media in part because of the grisly nature of her crime (murder by pickax) and partly because she was a pretty, photogenic white woman. Indeed, a new play, *Karla*, based on Tucker's crime, trial, and execution, opened in New York in October 2005. An example of an earlier but similarly famous case was that of Ruth Brown Snyder, who was executed in New York on January 12, 1928. An attending journalist surreptitiously photographed Snyder's execution in New York's electric chair, and that dramatic photograph appeared the next morning on the front page of the

Victor L. Streib, "Rare and Inconsistent: The Death Penalty for Women," *Fordham Urban Law Journal*, vol. 33, no. 2, January 2006, pp. 609–628. Copyright © 2006 *Fordham Urban Law Journal*. Reproduced by permission.

newspaper, destined to be reprinted many times subsequently. Journalistic descriptions of collections of numerous cases also abound, often tending to exploit them with lurid details.

We also have riveting films based on this theme. Some are built around real women's cases. The Florida case of Aileen Wuornos, executed on October 9, 2002, spawned several films. The best known was a semi-fictionalized account entitled *Monster*, released in 2003 and starring Charlize Theron, a role for which Theron received both a Golden Globe and Oscar. The Wuornos case had been the basis for earlier documentary films based upon her actual life. Nearly half a century ago, the 1958 film *I Want to Live* provided a reasonably accurate portrayal of the actual case of Barbara Graham, executed in California on June 6, 1955. In a precursor to Theron's recognition for her portrayal of Wuornos, actress Susan Hayward also won both a Golden Globe and an Oscar for her portrayal of Graham. Other films portray fictionalized women under sentences of death. One such example, *Last Dance*, released in 1996, starred Sharon Stone as a woman sentenced to death and actually executed. Based on a composite of several cases both real and fictional, Stone portrayed a condemned woman who evolves from a tough, foul-mouthed killer into a nurturing big sister and would-be lover before being executed.

Women account for about ten percent of murder arrests nationally.

But what of the rest of the women sentenced to death in the real world and, in some cases, actually executed? Who were they, and why were these extremely *rare* cases singled out to receive this ultimate punishment? Why are such women so commonly condemned but ignored by our death penalty system, by scholarly research on crime and the death penalty, and to some degree by the popular media? These questions have been asked by previous authors: "Few though their numbers may be, they are on death row, and for the most part terribly isolated, invisible, and alone." A[n] ... investigative report labels them "The Forgotten Population." Apparently a similar tendency to ignore such cases is true in Britain as well, where "their cases remain almost totally unknown." ...

Women Less Likely to Murder

We know that women are much less likely than men to commit murder, essentially the only crime currently that might result in a death sentence. In fact, women account for about ten percent of murder arrests nationally. At least some of these murder arrests occur, however, in jurisdictions that don't have the death penalty. In addition, certainly not all of the murders upon which these arrests are based are capital murders [punishable by the death penalty]. While we have fairly reliable data on the number of women arrested for murder in each jurisdiction during any one time period, these are only police data for their characterizations of the crimes committed. The data we do not have, however, would describe the number of these murders that were indeed capital murders, a determination made by prosecuting attorneys and not by the police. We also lack comprehensive, reliable data on the number of murder cases in which capital charges are filed by prosecutors, plea bargained to lesser charges, or actually brought to capital trials.

Coming out the other end of this long, dark tunnel of the early stages of the death penalty process, we do know that women account for only two percent of death sentences imposed at the trial level. This appears to be significant, in that ten percent of murder arrests were of women but only two percent of death sentences for murder are of women. The gender differential gets even worse: Women account for only 1.5 percent persons presently on death row and for only 1.1 percent of persons actually executed in this modern era (1973–present).

Execution of Women Killers

The actual execution of female offenders is quite rare, with only 568 instances in the 374 years from 1632 through 2005. These are documented cases of lawful executions of females and exclude lynchings and similar deaths imposed upon females. Beginning with the earliest American colonial period, these 568 female executions constitute about 2.8 percent of all American executions. Documenting the older executions of female offenders is quite challenging, but we do have fairly complete documentation of these executions since 1900. From 1900 through 2005, only 0.6 percent (50/8339) of all executions were of women. . . .

During the past 106 years, nineteen states and the federal government have executed female offenders. This was approximately half of the United States jurisdictions that had the death penalty during that time period. They ranged in age from seventeen-year-old Virginia Christian in Virginia to fifty-eight-year-old Louise Peete in California. In contrast, the entire northwest quarter of the United States has not seen any executions of female offenders since 1900. This northwest quarter consists of all states west of the Mississippi and north of the southern-most western states. These fifteen contiguous northwestern states are Colorado, Idaho, Iowa, Kansas, Minnesota, Missouri, Montana, Nebraska, Nevada, North Dakota, Oregon, South Dakota, Utah, Washington, and Wyoming. Twelve of these fifteen northwestern states (excluding only Minnesota, Missouri, and Nevada) have never executed any female offenders in their entire histories.

Comparing these post-1900 data with data from previous American eras reveals that this practice is even rarer now than it was in previous centuries. The current death penalty era began in 1973, even though it did not result in actual executions of any offenders until 1977. The previous death penalty era was terminated by the Supreme Court's 1972 decision in *Furman v. Georgia*, which in effect struck down all then-existing death penalty statutes. However, both Florida and Utah enacted new death penalty statutes before the end of 1972, and fifteen more states followed suit in 1973. For simplicity of comparison, this analysis marks the beginning as 1973, allowing for a period of six months following the *Furman* decision for the various jurisdictions to reconsider the death penalty. In 1976, the United States Supreme Court ruled that most of these early-1970s death penalty statutes were constitutional.

Actual executions began soon thereafter, with the first being that of Gary Mark Gilmore on January 17, 1977, in Utah. We finally saw executions of women offenders in 1984, and the last such execution as of this writing was of Frances Newton in Texas in 2005. . . .

Virginia, a leading death penalty state for male offenders, has imposed only one death sentence on a female offender since 1973.

Only eleven (1.1 percent) of the 1004 total executions from 1973 through 2005 have been of female offenders. This execution pace has changed recently, with only one (0.2 percent) of the 434 executions from 1973 to 1997 being a female offender. Since 1998, ten (1.8 percent) of the 570 total executions have been of female offenders. This recent (1998–2005) execution pace matches almost exactly that beginning in 1900, so it appears that the 1973–1997 lull in executions of female offenders was atypical and that we have now returned to our normal rate. Three women were executed in 2001, all in Oklahoma, the most executions nationally of women in any one year since 1953. The last woman executed, as of this writing, was Francis Newton in Texas on September 14, 2005.

Recent Death Sentences Imposed on Women

A total of 155 death sentences were imposed upon female offenders from 1973 through 2005. . . . These 155 death sentences for female offenders constitute only 2.1 percent of all death sentences during this period of thirty-three years. The typical annual death sentencing rate for female offenders during the last decade has been between two and seven sentences. The wide fluctuations in the number of women sentenced to death annually are unexplained by changes in statutes, court rulings, or public opinion.

These 155 death sentences for female offenders since 1973 have been imposed by twenty-five individual states and by the federal government, comprising well over half of the thirty-nine death penalty jurisdictions during this time period. The top five states (California, North Carolina, Florida, Texas, and Ohio) account for almost half of all such sentences since 1973. Virginia, a leading death penalty state for male offenders, has imposed only one death sentence on a female offender since 1973. Virginia last executed a female offender in 1912 (Virginia Christian, also the last juvenile female executed in the entire United States). . . .

The most obvious empirical conclusion to be drawn from these data is that this practice has been rare *and* inconsistent, *with little suggestion of it being grounded in a rational process.*

Women Currently on Death Row

Of the 155 death sentences imposed since 1973, only forty-nine women remained under sentences of death in seventeen states and under federal jurisdiction as of the end of 2005. . . .

Over one-quarter (thirteen out of forty-nine or twenty-seven percent) of these forty-nine female offenders killed their husbands or boyfriends; and almost one-quarter (ten out of forty-nine or twenty percent) killed their children, grandchildren, etc. Two additional women killed both their husbands and their children. The present ages of these forty-nine female offenders range from twenty-one to seventy-two years old, and they have been on death row from two weeks to nearly twenty years. . . .

Some of these women are on death row in states that have executed women in the current era, including Alabama (2002) and Texas (2005). Others are in states that have not engaged in this practice in some time, including California (1962) and Pennsylvania (1946). For still others of these states, the execution of female offenders is at most a distant memory, including Kentucky (1868) and Tennessee (1837). Two states, Idaho and Indiana, currently have women on death row but have never actually executed a female offender in their entire histories.

Recommendations to Make the Process Rational

The data presented and explored in this Article reveal the instances where the death penalty has been imposed on female offenders during at least the past century and in some cases for several centuries. The most obvious empirical conclusion to be drawn from these data is that this practice has been *rare* and *inconsistent*, with little suggestion of it being grounded in a rational process. Perhaps the most striking example comes from Oklahoma. That state has executed only four women in its history: one in 1903 and three in 2001. Nothing about the murder rate by women or the general use of the death penalty in Oklahoma explains why no such executions occurred prior to 1903 or in the near-century between 1903 and 2001. Texas, the clear leader in current executions, has executed well over 1,000 people in its history. Only six of these executions have been of women, however. Two women were executed in the 1850s and one in 1863, but the next Texas execution of a woman was in 1998, leaving a gap of 135 years between executions of women. Other states reflect similarly sporadic patterns.

The other obvious empirical conclusion is that no patterns can be found explaining (1) why certain women are sentenced to death and others are not, and (2) what criteria we use to select the women to be actually executed from those sentenced to death. Admittedly, the same questions can be raised about the death penalty for male offenders, but it appears that these maladies affect the death penalty for women even more acutely. Both of these empirical conclusions should lead us to seek a more rational, gender-neutral death penalty process.

The concerns raised about sex bias and disparate impact based upon sex are quite difficult to address. The author's earlier work provided several recommendations in this regard, but probably the most cogent are (1) to ask the appropriate legislatures to examine their death penalty statutes with these issues in mind, and (2) to implement the federal approach to instructing capital juries about sex bias and requiring written certification from those juries that sex bias was not a factor in their verdict. The first recommendation would require no more than a state-specific examination of death penalty statutes by a legislative committee and/or a special investigator. Such an examination could identify statutory provisions that might fall with different weight upon male and female offenders. The process could then move on to seek means to amend those statutory provisions to make them more gender-neutral.

One fears that a push toward gender neutrality in the death penalty system may fall more punitively on women than on men.

The second recommendation may do more to make us feel good than to implement any actual progress toward gender-neutrality, but at least it puts the issue on the table. A jury hearing a death penalty case in federal court is instructed by the trial court judge at the close of the sentencing that "it shall not consider the . . . sex of the defendant . . . and the jury is not to recommend a sentence of death unless it has concluded that it would recommend a sentence of death for the crime in question no matter what the . . . sex of the defendant . . . may be." And, if a death verdict is returned, each juror must sign a certificate that the sex of the offender was not considered in reaching that death verdict. Such provisions at least assure that capital jurors focus on the gender issue, even if we have no guarantee that they take the issue seriously.

In the end, one fears that a push toward gender neutrality in the death penalty system may fall more punitively on women than on men, or at least to be a mixed bag. That is, if female capital offenders appear to be screened out more often than male capital offenders, then one might solve this by sentencing more women to death and executing more of them once they are sentenced to death. If capital jurors were asked to avoid sex bias in their deliberations, they might be more likely to treat female defendants as if they were male than to treat male defendants as if they were female. Conversely, legislators might not be inclined to seek ways to execute more women, given the apparent lack of political, social, cultural, and religious support for such a policy. In fact, we may quietly support the premise that our harshest criminal justice process should take it easy on women.

Scientific Evidence Does Not Ensure Guilt in Death Penalty Cases

Sheila Jasanoff

Sheila Jasonoff is a professor of science and technology studies at the John F. Kennedy School of Government at Harvard University.

"Relying on Science, Romney Files Death Penalty Bill." With that headline, a press release on April 28, 2005 announced that Massachusetts Governor Mitt Romney was seeking to reintroduce by legislation the death penalty that the state's Supreme Judicial Court ruled unconstitutional in 1984. The remainder of the text left little doubt that science was a major basis for the governor's action. The press release quoted Romney as saying that the bill provided a "gold standard for the death penalty in the modern scientific age." Positing a symmetry that will be questioned below, Romney also declared, "Just as science can free the innocent, it can also identify the guilty." The bill itself deferred to science by calling for corroborating scientific evidence, multiple layers of review, and a novel "no doubt" standard of proof. By raising the required standard of evidence and by restricting the class of capital crimes, the proposed law hoped to correct the defects of other death penalty statutes. As Romney remarked to the press, "I'm hoping [Massachusetts lawmakers] take a look at this and say 'you know, this removes the major weakness in death penalty statutes in other states.' The weakness in the death penalty statutes in other states, of course, is the fear that you may execute someone who is innocent. *We remove that possibility*" (emphasis added). Most newspaper headlines re-

Sheila Jasanoff, "Just Evidence: The Limits of Science in the Legal Process," *Journal of Law, Medicine, & Ethics*, Summer 2006, pp. 328–341. Reproduced by permission.

porting on the bill, both before and after its introduction, flagged science as the factor most influencing Romney, and quoted his desire for incontrovertible, foolproof evidence.

The governor's faith in the perfectibility of the death penalty reflects modern societies' conviction that science can deliver failsafe, and therefore just, legal outcomes where the law, acting on its own, might fall short. That belief, in turn, owes much to the widely recognized self-corrective nature of science, which is thought to identify mistakes and weed out error more effectively than other social institutions. As the noted American sociologist of science, Robert K. Merton, observed in a 1942 article, "organized skepticism" is one of the distinctive norms of science. Implemented through the practices of peer review, this skeptical stance keeps scientists from accepting each other's results until they conform to communally negotiated standards of truth and objectivity. Merton argued that it is essential in the scientific community to aim for high standards of accuracy because scientists, who build on each other's work, have a collective stake in making their claims reliable and reproducible. Merton saw organized skepticism, as well as three other norms—communalism, universalism, and disinterestedness—as an institutional imperative of science.

Science in the Legal Arena

However, when science is used for legal purposes, it cannot be taken for granted that the same institutional imperatives continue to apply. In the legal arena, the context for science changes, and these changes affect the results one can expect from science. The law has its own institutional needs and constraints, and these are broadly geared toward ensuring that justice is done in each individual case. Processes designed to meet the law's primary imperatives are not necessarily well suited to discriminating between good and bad scientific claims; nor is it clear that the law does, or indeed always should, defer to science's overriding commitment to self-correction.

The U.S. Supreme Court attempted in 1993 to forge convergence between science and law in admissibility decisions for scientific expert evidence in federal trials. Trial judges, the Court held in the landmark case of *Daubert v. Merrell Dow Pharmaceuticals, Inc.*, should act, in effect, as surrogates for the scientific community in determining admissibility, and they should do so by applying the same standards that scientists would bring to the assessment of relevance and reliability. But it quickly became clear that the corrective processes that operate within science cannot be reproduced wholesale in legal settings. For example, in *General Electric Co. v. Joiner* the Court held that a trial judge's admissibility ruling can be reviewed by an appellate court only on grounds of abuse of discretion. This stringent review standard serves the law's interest in repose, by letting stand most trial court decisions, but it also insulates admissibility rulings against the kind of systematic peer skepticism that is routine in science.

Science enters the courtroom not in the form of bare facts or claimed truths about the world, but as evidence.

The use of scientific evidence such as DNA tests in court thus brings into collaboration two institutions with significantly different aims and normative commitments. In their by no means friction-free encounter, neither science nor law completely retains or completely relinquishes its autonomy. Science done to serve the law cannot proceed in quite the same ways as science done purely to advance the cause of science; and, while turning to science for authoritative input, the law never sets aside its commitment to core values beyond the search for factual accuracy. Lawmakers' expectations of science to simply step in and cure the law's deficiencies, without taking into account the disparate dynamics of the two institutions, are exaggerated (as in Romney's claim that his bill would "remove" the possibility of wrongful executions), and, at the limit, lead to questionable justice.

A starting point for creating a framework of more reasonable expectations for the relationship between law and science is to recognize that science enters the courtroom not in the form of bare facts or claimed truths about the world, but as *evidence*. That is, science must be worked into the particular kinds of propositions, representations, or material objects that the law regards as germane to establishing which party is telling the more plausible story. Scientific and technical evidence presented by expert witnesses, in particular, has to meet a number of criteria specific to the epistemological needs of the law. For instance, it must be relevant, it must be timely, and it must meet the *Daubert* tests of admissibility [of expert testimony]. This article examines points in the transition from scientific observation to proffered legal evidence at which problems may creep into the production of science for legal uses. . . .

Truth Differs in Science and Law

Scientific activity today is conducted under extremely diverse conditions to serve many different goals and purposes. As science has moved to tackle more and more complex aspects of natural and social behavior, it is not so much the idea of truth that has shifted as society's views of what should *count* as truth in particular frameworks of inquiry. Although all forms of scientific activity strive as far as possible to find correct answers to problems, the context in which an investigation is carried out necessarily affects the kinds of conclusions it reaches. For the most part, facts produced to serve the aims of litigation do not grow out of, nor play a part in, the same kinds of social interactions as do the facts produced in basic research science or even in regulatory science. Thus, the production of scientific facts needed to resolve legal conflicts differs in salient respects from the production of facts required to test a theory of consciousness, prove the safety of a drug, or assess the likely impacts of a pollutant on human health or ecosystems. Nor are findings in all these diverse domains held to the same standards of certainty or robustness. Without giving up on the truth in principle, scientists, judges, and policy-makers may legitimately differ in deciding what they will accept as factual enough to support the actions expected of them. Legal decisions rely not so much on whether a particular claimed fact is true, as on its relevance to the case at hand, and on how much it contributes to the strength and quality of the totality of the evidence. . . .

Scientific fact-finding in a sense always looks forward. . . . Legal fact-finding, by contrast, is backward-looking.

What counts as true for the law need not count as true for science, and in exceptional cases even scientific truths may not be accepted as valid for legal purposes. Three dimensions of difference are worthy of note, each reflecting underlying normative concerns that differentiate scientific from legal practice: first, the divergent roles of fact-finding in science and the law: second, the unequal need for certainty in scientific and legal contexts; and third, the disparate ethical constraints framing the production and use of knowledge in the two institutional settings.

Scientific Fact-Finding Is Forward-Looking

First, possibly the most salient difference between legally relevant facts and normal scientific facts is that the former are frequently specific to the cases they are supposed to illuminate, whereas the latter are expected to have more general validity. Scientific fact-finding in a sense always looks forward. Its aim is to advance the frontiers of knowledge in a given field, allowing future scientists to build on today's research. Legal fact-finding, by contrast, is backward-looking. Its purpose is to re-create as closely as possible something that happened in the past, to fill in the details of a story whose broad outlines are already known or suspected. Legal facts, whether based on science or not, seldom have a life outside the class of cases for which they were produced. Their function is not to serve as facts pure and simple, but rather as *evidence.*

To be sure, facts about causation ascertained in mass exposure cases—such as tobacco, asbestos or breast implant litigation—can affect the lives of large numbers of people and carry major economic and policy consequences. Research on such problems can even shed light on previously unstudied biological or biochemical processes, such as human immune system responses to environmentally induced mutations. In general, however, it is the very specificity of facts that makes them valuable for resolving legal disputes. Though general scientific principles can help rule out some causal stories as implausible, successful legal story-telling is never complete without facts particular to the case. Seen in this light, DNA profiling has proved so important to the legal system not only because it rests on generally accepted scientific principles of genetic variability, but also, and perhaps more importantly, because it claims to provide near-unique confirmations of identity in situations where identity would otherwise remain contested.

These differences in the function of facts means, in turn, that the social practices of fact-finding in science and law are not identical—and the differences may have important consequences for doing justice. Science generated to establish specific causation in lawsuits may never be subjected to the kind of ongoing communal scrutiny that characterizes normal research science. Unless the stakes are large, as in mass tort cases, facts developed for litigation may not be peer reviewed or published. Replication, which many see as the ultimate test of truth in science, is equally improbable because the questions posed to forensic science are rarely of great concern to the scientific community at large. Whether or not DNA tests conclusively showed that Nicole Simpson's blood was found in O.J. Simpson's bedroom will never arouse general scientific interest, any more than whether the glove found at the crime scene fit Simpson's hand or it was his size ten, Bruno Magli shoe that left a tell-tale footprint [Simpson was tried for the 1994 murder of his wife, Nicole, and her friend.]

Quality Control of Scientific Evidence

For litigation-relevant science, efforts at quality control must therefore be, on the whole, front-ended—that is, they must be built into fact-finding processes in advance rather than left to be sorted out on a timeline independent of the flow of litigation. The Massachusetts capital punishment council tacitly recognized this problem when it recommended multiple layers of review to assure the quality of the scientific evidence in capital cases. The evidentiary gold standard incorporated into the Romney bill, however, struck even the Council as extremely expensive. The report noted that the costs would be tolerable because they would be incurred for only a small number of death eligible cases. Others, however, questioned whether scarce law enforcement resources should be directed toward flushing out error in a tiny handful of cases, and whether adequate resources would be allocated to upgrade crime labs to standards needed for producing high-quality evidence.

The idea that science can be relied on to produce fool-proof verdicts ... is both ethically and practically questionable.

Second, cost is not the only factor that makes the law accept facts that science might still deem provisional. Delay is another important consideration, and not simply because lengthy proceedings entail costs to the system. Scientific facts needed to resolve legal disputes frequently come into being only as those disputes unfold. They are not available before the fact in some convenient storehouse of relevant, well-documented, yet case-specific facts. On the principle that justice delayed is justice denied, it is unfair to expect plaintiffs to wait until all the uncertainties associated with their claims have been definitively ironed out. Legally, in any case, scientific claims are admitted into court not in consequences of their facticity *per se*—that is, not because of their likely correspondence to an external, natural truth—but because they are relevant to a story about human actions and motivations. Not surprisingly, then, the standard of certainty that litigants have to meet in order to win their case is different from the standard of certainty needed to establish the truth of a scientific fact. In civil cases, plaintiffs need only demonstrate by a preponderance of the evidence that their version of the case is more likely than not to be true. In criminal cases, the defendant needs the quantum of evidence that produces a reasonable doubt in the jury's mind in order to be acquitted. Legal evidence, in other words, need not and should not be held to scientific standards of robustness.

Science and the Death Penalty

Third, the idea that science can be relied on to produce foolproof verdicts, as Romney's support for the death penalty strongly implied, is both ethically and practically questionable. The record of capital punishment in the United States shows that it is overwhelmingly the poor, the disadvantaged, and the racially marked who are actually executed. The most important reason for this stratification in the meting out of death is that money determines the quality of legal representation. Poor defendants, it seems clear, suffer twice: first, in being socialized into conditions that are more likely to encourage violent crime: and second, in lacking the resources with which to mount a convincing defense. The application of a "no doubt" standard, such as that proposed in the Romney bill, misleadingly implies that even the most lingering doubts about guilt can be dispelled through stringent legal and scientific quality control. In practice, the degree of doubt in a juror's mind depends on an advocate's success or failure in arousing or allaying misgivings, whether about the heinousness of the crime or about the nature of the evidence, or both. Forensic science, in other words, cannot rule out doubt on its own, but only as it is represented, and contested, in court, as a component of a larger story. Well-paid lawyers defending wealthy clients tend to be more diligent in deconstructing weaknesses in the prosecution's incriminating evidence. Indigent defendants, who cannot afford effective lawyering, may find their facts decided less by the strength of the scientific evidence as assessed by technical experts than by the vigor and ingenuity of the advocacy mobilized in their defense.

Science and Settlements

Finally, social policies favoring certain types of settlements may sometimes militate against an all-out reliance on science. For example, under U.S. state laws governing parentage, a child born in wedlock is presumed to be the biological offspring of both members of the married couple. While DNA tests may be used to disapprove paternity, some states have imposed a two- or three-year statute of limitations on such demonstrations. After that time, it becomes irrelevant whether paternity tests reveal the husband not to be the child's natural father: the stability of the family unit matters more to the state than the truth of biological parentage. Some U.S. courts have denied prisoners' requests for post-conviction DNA testing on the ground that this would violate the law's interest in finality, allowing technological progress to undermine legal settlements. Important support for this position comes from a 1993 Supreme Court decision, *Herrera v. Collins*, which held that a claim of actual innocence is not enough to reopen a criminal conviction based on a fair trial: the prisoner, who is no longer entitled to a presumption of innocence, must also show constitutional error. In both contexts, the law's concern for social order overrides what science deems to be the facts of the matter. The social truth of what constitutes a family and what amounts to justice in the eyes of the law operates in these cases independently of scientific truths concerning human reproduction or genetic identity. One may consider such divergences between science and law to be arbitrary, even unjust, but it is important to recognize that they are rooted in institutional logics that are not and need not be the same. Necessarily, then, there cannot be any neat one-to-one mapping between scientific truth and legal evidence based on science. . . .

Science Is Context-Specific

Scientific truth-making, in particular, as human beings engage in it, is always a social enterprise. It is situated in particular places and circumstances; it is context-specific, purposive, and culturally embedded. As such, even scientific claims are subject to distortion, through imperfections in the very human systems that produced them. In attempting to render justice, the law's objective should be, in part, to restore to view these potential shortcomings, instead or uncritically taking on board a decontextualized image of science that ignores its social and institutional dimensions. Doing justice, after all, demands a complex balancing of multiple considerations, in an analytic framework that keeps social contexts firmly within view while constructing compelling narratives of cause and blame. When science enters the courtroom, it should do so as an adjunct to the law's need for credible but meaningful story-telling. In a court of law, science cannot hold itself out as simply science, the source of transcendental truths; more modestly, and with appropriate caveats, it can be the source of just evidence.

The Evidence of Innocence Is Often Withheld in Death Penalty Cases

Dale S. Recinella

Dale S. Recinella is an attorney, an author, and an expert on the death penalty and how it impacts religion and ethics.

As I begin my seventh year of cell-to-cell ministry on Florida's death row, it is not surprising that I am frequently asked to speak to Catholic audiences on the realities of the American death penalty. Most invitations are from Catholics who are sincerely interested in the truth, but who know that politicians and agenda-oriented media channels have provided them only opinions, with almost no facts. In such an environment, our dialogue must start with the basics. Paragraph 2267 of the *Catechism of the Catholic Church* is the relevant passage on Catholic teaching about the death penalty:

> Assuming that the guilty party's identity and responsibility have been fully determined, the traditional teaching of the Church does not exclude recourse to the death penalty, if this is the only possible way of effectively defending human lives against the unjust aggressor.

> If, however, non-lethal means are sufficient to defend and protect people's safety from the aggressor, authority will limit itself to such means, as these are more in keeping with the concrete conditions of the common good and more in conformity with the dignity of the human person.

> Today, in fact, as a consequence of the possibilities which the state has for effectively preventing crime, by rendering

one who has committed an offense incapable of doing harm—without definitively taking away from him the possibility of redeeming himself—the cases in which the execution of the offender is an absolute necessity "are very rare, if not practically non-existent."

A Theological Debate

It has been disappointing to find that two of the questions most frequently asked of me about this text add very little to the audiences' understanding of the issues. The first question focuses on the last paragraph of the catechism text and is usually asked by liberals: "Isn't it true that the Catholic Church has changed its teaching about capital punishment?" I have learned that this is not so much a question about capital punishment as an attempt to suggest something about the doctrine of infallibility—namely that any change in this teaching proves the doctrine is questionable. The response, of course, is that the teaching is consistent, but nuanced to take into account modern realities.

America's death penalty . . . is deeply flawed, fallible and sometimes perverted.

A second frequent question focuses upon the middle of the first paragraph and is usually asked by conservatives: "Isn't it true that the death penalty is not intrinsically evil but abortion is?" This is usually not a death penalty question, but rather a thinly veiled assertion that real Catholics can support only a particular political party. That issue has been addressed in a statement by our U.S. Catholic bishops.

The point for our purposes is that both questions are salvos in an esoteric theological debate, which assumes, for purposes of argument, that the death penalty works flawlessly and infallibly. No one in America has ever seen such a death penalty. Neither question advances the knowledge of the average

American Catholic parishioner about the deep moral and ethical problems with America's death penalty, which is a deeply flawed, fallible and sometimes perverted system.

A much more significant question leaps from the introduction to the catechism text. "Does the American death penalty guarantee a full determination of the accused party's identity and responsibility?" The answer is a resounding no. There are many factors that contribute to this result. Perhaps the most severe is the American legal doctrine of what is called procedural bar.

Procedural Bar

Procedural bar is a legal concept that has been marketed to the public under false pretenses. Americans are told that there is no reason why it should take longer than five years after a death sentence to carry out an execution. Therefore, we are advised, anyone on death row for longer than five years must be clogging the courts with spurious appeals. The solution is simply to cut off access to the courts after a certain period of time. That is the doctrine. After a certain period of time, in other words, the accused is forbidden to present new evidence to the courts.

In Florida, a condemned man may introduce evidence of innocence only within one to two years after the imposition of the death sentence.

The foregoing pretenses fly in the face of reality. Since 1976, according to the non-profit Death Penalty Information Center in Washington, D.C., 115 people have been released from America's death rows with evidence of their innocence. For those 115 exonerated death row inmates, the average time between being sentenced to death and exoneration was more than nine years.

So one might assume that when a citizen's life is at stake, the time periods allowed for the introduction of new evidence would be long ones. Not so. In Florida, a condemned man may introduce evidence of innocence only within one to two years after the imposition of the death sentence. In Texas, the condemned can do so only within 18 months after receiving a death sentence. In Virginia the period has been temporarily extended from 21 days to 90 days.

What about evidence of innocence that the prosecutors and police had in their possession but hid from the court? Too bad. Thanks to various legal procedures, prosecutors have been able to obtain court decisions to the effect that such conduct no longer merits court review of innocence. Politically desirable executions can roll forward, enhancing the political careers, salaries and perks of ambitious politicians and government employees, unimpeded by the evidence of innocence that may be sitting in the courthouse basement—never to be reviewed by a judge or a jury.

We might hope that in the United States only trivial evidence would be disregarded in this fashion. If only that were true. Unfortunately, it is not. For example, in one case the prosecution "hid" the original police report and used a "revised" police report at trial. The original police report did not support the guilt of the accused; the revised police report did. No jury or court has been able to review the original police report. Too much time has passed; the evidence of innocence is thus subject to procedural bar.

The Anti-Terrorism and Effective Death Penalty Act of 1996 severely limits the ability of federal courts to hear post-trial evidence of innocence.

Recently, in Missouri the state argued, almost successfully, that there is no constitutional right not to be executed just because one is innocent. In that case, a man had been sentenced to death based on nothing but the testimony of three jail-house snitches. Years later, all three admitted to lying. The Missouri State Supreme Court ruled for a new trial by a razor-thin vote of 4 to 3.

Federal Courts Are Not Safety Nets

We might want to believe that the federal courts would act as a safety net against execution of the innocent. Not anymore. The Anti-Terrorism and Effective Death Penalty Act of 1996 severely limits the ability of federal courts to hear post-trial evidence of innocence that state courts have refused to consider. The shortened time limits created by this law pose an especially egregious risk of executing poor defendants despite late-discovered evidence of innocence. Without the resources to hire an attorney, they may be unable to meet the shorter time limits.

Even those with competent counsel are out of luck. Recently, a federal court took the rare step of granting a state death row inmate a new trial. The federal judge was outraged that the prosecutor had materially misled the court and the jury about the motivations of the state's only witness. It had been misrepresented to them that the witness had nothing to gain by his testimony, when in fact he was being released from reams of felony charges. The state also hid other evidence concerning their star witness, who, it turns out, had himself originally been charged with the murder. The state's own attorneys told the press that there was not a shred of evidence connecting the death row inmate to the murder. Then the federal appeals court overruled the new trial and reinstated the death penalty. Why? It had been too long. Procedural bar. The state is pushing on toward execution.

America's Plunge Toward Routine Executions

The watershed event in America's plunge toward routine executions without a full determination of the condemned's identity and responsibility was the U.S. Supreme Court case of Leonel Herrera in 1993. A former Texas judge submitted an affidavit stating that another man had confessed to the crime for which Herrera was facing execution. Numerous other pieces of new evidence also threw doubt on his conviction. In a modern rendition of the famous Gospel scene of Pilate's hand-washing, the Supreme Court announced that it could not be concerned with factual innocence. It could address only procedural violations. Herrera was executed.

This is the death penalty in the United States. This is the disastrous state of affairs that caused Governor George H. Ryan Sr. to commute the sentences of everyone on Illinois' death row. This is the mess that prompted pro-death penalty Governor Frank Keating of Oklahoma to opine that our standard of guilt must be raised from "beyond a reasonable doubt" to "moral certainty." Under the American death penalty, it is preposterous to assume that the guilty party's identity and responsibility have been fully determined, as required by the *Catholic Catechism.*

Although we may not yet be ready to tackle the abstract theological concepts involved in the abolition of the death penalty universally, we can say with certainty that all American Catholics who accept church teaching must be opposed to the death penalty as it is used in the United States today. Until the case of Leonel Herrera is overturned, the Anti-Terrorism and Effective Death Penalty Act of 1996 is repealed, and the legal doctrine of procedural bar is banned in capital cases, it is simply not possible to be a faithful Catholic and support the use of the death penalty in the United States.

CHAPTER 3

Is Capital Punishment an Effective Deterrent to Crime?

Chapter Preface

Since Maryland reestablished capital punishment in 1978, it has executed five people and set one convicted man free when his innocence was discovered. State law provides that those convicted of first-degree murder are eligible for the death penalty if prosecutors can prove at least one of ten aggravating factors, including murdering a law enforcement officer, kidnapping the victim, or committing murder while in prison.

For several years, Maryland has been embroiled in a bitter debate over its death penalty statute. The issue rose to prominence in 2002 when then-governor Parris Glendening, a Democrat, imposed a moratorium on the death penalty so that racial disparity and other issues could be examined. His successor, Robert L. Ehrlich Jr., a Republican, lifted the ban. In December 2006 the Maryland Court of Appeals ruled that the state's procedure for carrying out lethal injections was adopted improperly, a defect that the court ordered must be rectified before any more death row inmates were executed. The unanimous ruling by the court of appeals moved the debate squarely into the political realm, where Governor Ehrlich Jr., at the request of incoming Governor Martin O'Malley, left the issue for his Democratic successor. Under the new administration, Maryland faces three choices: fix the regulations ordered by the court, let the moratorium stand, or repeal the death penalty.

In March 2007 Governor O'Malley testified before both a state Senate and House legislative committee. He urged lawmakers to repeal the death penalty. The governor argued that the elected bodies should revoke the statute because it does not serve as deterrent to murder. He also maintained that capital punishment may actually act as an accelerant to murder. According to the governor, in 2005 the murder rate in death penalty states was 46 percent higher than in states without it. The murder rates between death penalty states and non-death penalty states had been about the same in 1990. Moreover, murder rates declined by 56 percent in states without the death penalty, compared to a decline of only 38 percent in states with it. Governor O'Malley also asserted that it costs the state over $400,000 more to prosecute a death penalty defendant than to imprison the same individual for life. Since 1978, Maryland has sentenced fifty-six people to death, costing taxpayers around $22.4 million in additional expenses. This revenue could have paid for five hundred additional police officers or provided drug treatment for ten thousand state residents. Unlike the death penalty, the governor believes that these "investments" save lives and are proven methods of deterring violent crime. In conclusion, the governor declared,

> And if the death penalty as applied is inherently unjust and lacks a deterrent value, we are left to ask whether the value to society of partial retribution outweighs the cost of maintaining capital punishment. While I am mindful of and sensitive to the closure (and in some cases the comfort) that the death penalty brings to the unfathomable pain of families that have lost loved ones to violent crime, I believe that is does not.

> Human dignity is the concept that leads brave individuals to sacrifice their lives for the lives of strangers. Human dignity is the universal truth that is the basis of ethics. Human dignity is the fundamental belief on which the laws of this state and this republic are founded. And absent a deterrent value, the damage done to the concept of human dignity by our conscious communal use of the death penalty is greater than the benefit of even a justly drawn retribution.

The governor's plea fell on mostly deaf ears, as both legislative chambers effectively voted down measures to repeal the death penalty. O'Malley, however, can continue the court-imposed death penalty moratorium as long as he remains in office.

Capital Punishment Does in Fact Deter Crime

Joanna M. Shepherd

Joanna M. Shepherd is a professor of law at Emory University School of Law in Atlanta, Georgia.

Chairman [Howard] Coble, Ranking Member [Robert C.] Scott and Members of the Subcommittee, thank you for having me here today to discuss the issues relating to H.R. 2934. As a Ph.D. Economist, the primary focus of my research has been the empirical analysis of crime. I have studied the deterrent effect of capital punishment extensively. I have three published studies on the topic and I am currently working on another study and a book.

Today I am going to briefly speak about three things: First I will speak on the early studies on whether capital punishment had a deterrent effect. The studies produced mixed results. Some found deterrence and others did not. Second, I will describe the modern studies from the past decade including my own studies. There have been 13 modern economic studies on the deterrent effect of capital punishment. All find that executions significantly deter murders. Finally, I will discuss what existing studies might be able to tell us about whether capital punishment could deter terrorism. Let me add that this testimony will only address deterrence. It will not consider any of the other possible issues of capital punishment such as moral problems, the socioeconomic patterns of who is executed or the dangers of executing innocent people.

Early Studies on Deterrence

First the early studies: The debate and the economics literature began with [economist] Isaac Ehrlich's two papers in the

Joanna M. Shepherd, hearing before the Subcommittee on Crime, Terrorism, and Homeland Security of the Committee on the Judiciary House of Representatives, 108th Congress, second session on H.R. 2934, April 21, 2004.

1970's. Ehrlich was the first to study capital punishment's deterrent effect using multivariate regression analysis. Multivariate regression analysis allowed Ehrlich to separate the effects on murder of many different factors such as the racial and age composition of the population, average income, unemployment, and the execution rate. Ehrlich's first paper used time series analysis, 36 years of overall U.S. data from 1933 to 1969. His second paper used cross-section analysis, 1 year of data from all 50 states.

All categories of murder are deterred by the death penalty, even so-called crimes of passion.

Both of Ehrlich's studies found significant deterrent effects. In fact, he estimated each execution resulted in about 8 fewer murders. Ehrlich's finding was controversial and loosed a flood of interest in statistical analysis of capital punishment. The papers that immediately followed Ehrlich used his original data or slight extensions and slightly different statistical methods. Many found that executions deter murder but others did not. The results were mixed. However, almost all of the early studies suffered from major flaws because they either used time series data or cross-section data. For technical reasons that economists agree on, these types of data are imperfect for measuring deterrence. The techniques have become obsolete in situations where better panel data are available.

Modern Studies on Deterrence

Panel data are data from several units like the 50 States or all U.S. counties over several years. Panel data techniques fix many of the problems associated with the data that early studies used. Now let's talk about the modern studies. 13 economic studies on capital punishment's deterrent effect have been conducted in the past decade. Most use new improved panel data and modern statistical techniques. They all use multivariate regression analysis to separate the effect on murder, of executions, demographics, economic factors, et cetera.

The studies are unanimous. All 13 of them find a deterrent effect. I have conducted three of these studies. My first study used 20 years of data from all U.S. counties to measure the effect of county differences on murder. My second paper used monthly data from all U.S. States for 22 years to measure the short-term effect of capital punishment. This paper also looks at different categories of murder to determine which kinds of murder are deterred by executions. The third study looks at the effect on murders of the 1970's Supreme Court moratorium on executions. All of my papers find a deterrent effect.

Moreover, I find that all categories of murder are deterred by the death penalty, even so-called crimes of passion. My results predict that each execution deters somewhere between 3 and 18 murders. The other 10 modern economics papers used different methods and different data than my own, but all find a significant deterrent effect.

Capital Punishment May Deter Terrorism

Finally, let's talk about what if anything the studies might be able to tell us about whether capital punishment deters terrorism. Unfortunately, there is not yet any empirical research specifically on capital punishment and terrorism. Some people might think that all terrorists are undeterrable fanatics. In fact, it might even be suggested that capital punishment could increase terrorism if potential terrorists view executions as their ticket to holy martyrdom.

If executions are a harsher penalty, then some terrorists should be deterred by them.

However, the indirect evidence from the other studies suggest that this may not be the case for three reasons: First, research shows that capital punishment deters every kind of murder that has been studied. This includes many kinds of murderers like terrorists who might not seem to be deterrable. My own paper found the death penalty has a deterrent effect on all categories of murder including crimes of passion and intimate murders that many people think are undeterrable. Second, capital punishment could have an overall deterrent effect on terrorism even if many terrorists are not influenced by capital punishment. To give a deterrent effect, all that is necessary is that a small fraction of terrorists are deterred. Obviously, the death penalty does not deter all murders, but it does deter a small important fraction of them. Third, although there are exceptions, news accounts . . . are replete with accounts of alleged terrorists who fight strenuously in court to get life imprisonment instead of the death penalty. These terrorists obviously view executions as a worse penalty than life in prison. If executions are a harsher penalty, then some terrorists should be deterred by them. Thanks again for having me, and I look forward to answering any questions you may have.

Homicidal Violence in Great Britain Has Increased Since the Abolition of the Death Penalty

Theodore Dalrymple

Theodore Dalrymple is a retired prison psychiatrist and a contributing editor of City Journal.

Anyone who watched Saddam Hussein being led to the gallows without any knowledge of who he was would have concluded that a dignified, decent, and upright man was being informally executed by a gang of criminals. After all, it was he, not they, who showed his face to the world; he, not they, who refused to disguise himself.

And the revelation that he was taunted by his gaolers immediately before his execution, and not allowed to sleep the previous night, has rendered his execution less than optimal, from the public-relations point of view. Anything he might have suffered as a result of mistreatment was, of course, trivial by comparison with the suffering he inflicted on thousands, perhaps millions, of others; but a sense of proportion in moral outrage has never been among the Middle East's great cultural virtues.

European Elite Is Against Death Penalty

The same, alas, is now true of Europe, or of the European official class and its tame intelligentsia. Everyone was agreed, of course, that Saddam was a very bad thing, a dictator who used every method of political persuasion from torture to a bullet in the neck and poison gas. But very few missed the opportunity to express an unctuous self-righteousness about the death penalty.

European leaders are so entirely, parochially, and narrow-mindedly enclosed within their own worldview that they are now unable to conceive of any opinion but their own.

The editorial of *Le Monde* on the day following, for example, was entitled "No to the Death Penalty," and said that while President [George W.] Bush may have claimed that the execution was a step on the path to democracy, "our," that is to say the French and superior, concept of democracy was different. The British foreign secretary and Irish foreign minister took the opportunity to express British and Irish opposition to the death penalty; the position of the Italian prime minister was even stronger (or weaker, depending on how you look at it); the Vatican also took the opportunity to express its opposition to the death penalty; and the European commissioner for foreign aid, M. Louis Michel, former foreign minister of that land of irreproachable integrity, Belgium, said, "You don't fight barbarism with acts that I deem as barbaric. The death penalty is not compatible with democracy."

In general, Europeans of the official class spoke as if the death penalty had been abolished in Europe in about 479 b.c., when it was abolished in Britain in 1965 and in France in 1981, not exactly historical epochs ago, even in the baby boomers' truncated historical perspective. Whatever the practical political consequences of the execution of Saddam, which are inherently uncertain, the fact is that the European leaders are so entirely, parochially, and narrow-mindedly enclosed within their own worldview that they are now unable to conceive of any opinion but their own.

The egregious M. Michel seems to be implying that the two largest and most important democracies in the world, the

U.S.A. and India, cannot actually be democracies at all because they have the death penalty. He also seems to be saying that New Zealand, Britain, Australia, Canada, and France were not democracies until 1961, 1965, 1973, 1976, and 1981, an odd reading of history, to say the least. Such is the ignorant arrogance of the great ones of Europe, who must have been confirmed in their decision not to allow any kind of democratic intervention in their deliberations by learning that in fact a clear majority of Europeans believed that Saddam ought to have been executed. If that is what people think, they clearly ought to be abolished.

Homicide Rate in Great Britain

The self-righteousness of the leaders was such that they seem totally unaware that there are any arguments in favor of the death penalty, and this is so whether or not you actually agree with the penalty.

Let us take Britain as an example. The homicide rate has doubled since the abolition, but the rate of homicidal violence has increased by up to ten times, if an American study is correct that improvements in trauma medicine have reduced the death rate from such violence by four-fifths. Moreover, the type of killings that would once have attracted the death penalty—for the majority of homicides were never punished by the death penalty in Britain—has increased disproportionately.

If the deterrent effect were only 2 percent, it would save 16 lives per year.

In Britain, at least 139 homicides have been committed since the abolition of the death penalty by people released after serving prison sentences for homicide. A further 98 killings have been perpetrated by people on parole for some lesser crime, in the last two years alone. While this is not directly relevant to the question of capital punishment, the abolition of the supreme penalty necessarily renders the whole criminal justice system less severe (the fitness of the punishment to the crime has to be sealed down proportionately), and it is difficult to believe that the vastly greater willingness of the population in Britain to commit acts of great violence is completely unrelated to this fact.

The effectiveness of the death penalty as a deterrent would have to be only very slight for it to be worthwhile from the point of view of saving lives. In the last 65 years of the penalty in Britain, about 13 people were hanged per year. If the deterrent effect were only 2 percent, it would save 16 lives per year. Moreover, the lives lost on one hand would be those of murderers, and on the other of the victims of murderers. It seems to me to be carrying the principle of all being born equal a little far if we don't prefer to save the lives of victims rather than those of perpetrators—assuming, of course, that the deterrent rate of 2 percent is real.

Lack of Moral Outrage for Victims

One of the principal, and best, arguments against the death penalty is the possibility of error. And of course to be done to death wrongly by the state is a terrible thing. But I have always been struck by the disparity between the outrage caused by errors committed by what, after all, is due process, all human institutions being fallible, and the outrage caused by killings committed by previously convicted killers.

Although I have not investigated the matter myself, I have been told by two people who have investigated it closely that there were five judicial errors in the last 65 years of the death penalty in Britain. Let us multiply by ten, to be on the safe side. This would still be only 36 percent of the number of people killed by already-convicted killers in a period of time only 63 percent as long.

A single case is, perhaps, emblematic. Recently, a 34-year-old man was convicted of murder after burning down the house of his 16-year-old former girlfriend, who no longer wished to see him, in the process killing not only her, but her brother, sister, and stepfather. A few months before, he had been released from prison after serving three and a half years of a seven-year sentence for having bashed in the skull of a woman who refused to leave her husband for him, fracturing it in seven places. This appalling case aroused no echo whatsoever in the intelligentsia, so tender for the rights of Saddam, even though the man's personal tally was equal to that of the entire judicial system over 65 years—that is, if my informants with regard to the errors are to be believed.

None of this is decisive. Even if the death penalty could be proved beyond all doubt to be a deterrent, it would still be open to opponents of the penalty to argue the deontological case that the state must never take life. But this would require perfectly consistent pacifism, which not many of our leaders adhere to. Even [Italian prime minister] St. Romano Prodi, would probably expect his bodyguards to shoot to kill if someone were about to throw a bomb at him—and this without due process.

I am not arguing that the death penalty is right; I am arguing that there is a serious case in its favor.

Moreover, it is important for deontologists among abolitionists to realize that a deontological argument can be put on the other side: that it is the duty of the state to maintain the death penalty, irrespective of its practical effects, because it has no right to extend mercy to brutal killers who are without extenuating circumstances.

I am not arguing that the death penalty is right; I am arguing that there is a serious case in its favor. This being so, European politicians have no business preening themselves on their moral superiority to everyone else, including in many cases their own electorates. It is dishonest to pretend that there is nothing to be said on the question opposite the side they take, and that only primitives and scoundrels do so. But then dishonesty makes the careers of such politicians, and not just their careers; it is, as the French say, their *métier*.

Hanging Saddam Hussein Will Deter Future Chaos in Iraq

Patrick Poole

Patrick Poole is an occasional contributor to American Thinker. *He maintains a blog called* Existential Space.

[Editor's Note: Saddam Hussein was hanged in December 2006.]

The news that Saddam Hussein has lost his final legal appeal and that he will be hanged sometime within the next 30 days [January 2007] should be welcome news for war-weary Americans. Thus, Saddam will receive the just punishment for his crimes against humanity that Adolf Hitler avoided with a suicide's bullet in the closing days of World War II.

Of course, the Human Rights Watch crowd has already begun the drumbeat about how brutal and inhumane such a punishment will be and have complained about how the trial was unfair. The trolls of *Daily Kos* and *Democratic Underground* are echoing this theme by tying the "inhumanity" of this verdict to the supposed immorality of "George Bush's War."

The Death Penalty Is a Right

To get lost in the cobwebs of the mind of the Left is to obscure the real issues here. We should remember that even in America, defendants are entitled to a fair trial, not a perfect trial. No perfection exists as long as there are humans involved. But the reason why Saddam Hussein must hang is because we value his rights as a human being and we recognize that he too—no matter how despicable his conduct and how

"Why Saddam Must Hang," *American Thinker*, December 29, 2006. www.american thinker.com. Reproduced by permission.

horrible his crimes—was created in the image of God. To deny him the hangman's noose is to say that he—and all of us for that matter—is leas than a human.

When we cease to consider what the criminal deserves and consider only what will cure him . . . we have tacitly removed him from the sphere of justice altogether.

This point of punishing a man to remind him and us that he is a man is lost on those who believe that man is merely an animal and who reject any notion of sin as outdated and mentally deranged. The British author C.S. Lewis addressed many years ago the practical consequences of the therapeutic approach to crime that underlies many of the arguments offered by Saddam's defenders. This approach which rejects any notion of retribution or of desert in proscribing punishment, is the subject of Lewis' short essay, "The Humanitarian Theory of Punishment" (now found in his collection of essays, *God in the Dock*). He describes the theory in this way:

> According to the Humanitarian theory, to punish a man because he deserves it, and as much as he deserves it, is mere revenge, and, therefore, barbarous and immoral. It is maintained that the only legitimate motives for punishing are the desire to deter others by example or to mend the criminal. When this theory is combined, as frequently happens, with the belief that all crime is more or less pathological, the idea of mending tails off into that of healing or curing and punishment becomes therapeutic. Thus is appears at first sight that we have passed from the harsh and self-righteous notion of giving the wicked their deserts to the charitable and enlightened one of tending the psychologically sick. What could be more amiable?

But Lewis identifies the utter inhumanity of this theory:

> My contention is that this doctrine, merciful though it appears, really means that each one of us, from the moment

he breaks the law, is deprived of the rights of a human being ... when we cease to consider what the criminal deserves and consider only what will cure him or deter others, we have tacitly removed him from the sphere of justice altogether; instead of a person, a subject of rights, we now have a mere object, a patient, a "case" ... But to be punished, however severely, because we have deserved it, because we "ought to have known better", is to be treated as a human person in God's image.

Loss of Objective Legal Standards

In the rest of his essay, Lewis identifies the practical outworking of the Humanitarian Theory of Punishment: gone are the objective standards of the law, replaced instead with the subjective assessments of psychologists and therapists; and the nexus between Justice and Mercy is effectively severed, making the whole system an unmerciful instrument of inhumanity.

The Humanitarian Theory of Justice advanced by organizations like Human Rights Watch destroys, not defends, human rights because it is predicated on treating all of use as subjects, not as men.

Under this view, punishment is not imposed on the basis on the just deserts of the individual and his responsibility to his fellow man, but the collective goals of society. This sets up a utilitarian scenario of an innocent man being punished if society (and more accurately, society's masters) believe it will benefit the public good. This, of course, is what we are seeing in the ongoing Duke [University] rape case, where young privileged white men are being put through the legal ringer to atone for the supposed iniquities of a racist white society, not on the basis of whether they actually committed the crime or not. And there are many people in that community who have no problem making these innocent kids pay, even knowing now that the evidence nowhere comes close to supporting their guilt.

Lewis also describes in frightening detail how the Humanitarian Theory of Punishment would play right into the hands of a tyrant:

> For if crime and disease are to be regarded as the same thing, it follows that any state of mind which our masters choose to call "disease" can be treated as crime; and compulsorily cured. It will be vain to plead that states of mind which displease government need not always involve moral turpitude and do not therefore always deserve forfeiture of liberty. For our masters will not be using the concepts of Desert and Punishment but those of disease and cure. We know that one school of psychology already regards religion as a neurosis. When this particular neurosis becomes inconvenient to government, what is to hind government from proceeding to "cure" it? Such "cure" will, of course, be compulsory; but under the Humanitarian theory it will not be called by the shocking name of Persecution. No one will blame us for being Christians, no one will hate us, no one will revile us. The new Nero will approach us with the silky manners of a doctor, and though all will be in fact as compulsory as the *tunica molesta* or Smithfield or Tyburn, all will go on within the unemotional therapeutic sphere where words like "right" and "wrong" or "freedom" and "slavery" are never heard. And thus when the command is given, every prominent Christian in the land may vanish overnight into Institutions for the Treatment of the Ideologically Unsound, and it will rest with the expert gaolers to say when (if ever) they are to re-emerge. But it will not be persecution. Even if the treatment is painful, even if it is life-long, even if it is fatal, that will be only a regrettable accident; the intention was purely therapeutic.

Human Rights Groups Destroys Rights

Anyone believing that Saddam's life should be spared would do well to read Lewis' penetrating critique of their worldview. The Humanitarian Theory of Justice advanced by organizations like Human Rights Watch destroys, not defends, human rights because it is predicated on treating all of us as subjects, not as men.

We should hang Saddam so that the world may know that as a responsible man with free will, he really was his brother's keeper.

Those condemning Saddam Hussein's sentence of death but still deploring his actions, rather than seeing how closely his depravity is to theirs, would rather identify him as a monster (excepting those 9/11 Truthers who believe that he never committed the crimes he was accused of) to avoid looking into the moral mirror. In that case, what blame can be attached to an animal that is merely acting according to its nature? As Elton John tells us, it's the Circle of Life! What kind of society is possible when men are allowed to indulge and gratify their basest desires? Doesn't it look very much like the utter chaos and grotesque brutality found everyday on the streets of Baghdad? Say whatever you will about the presence of American troops in Iraq, but make no mistake that it is solely the presence of those troops that is preventing a bloodbath the world hasn't seen since Rwanda.

Saddam Must Be Held to Account

And it is Saddam's regime that has bred this culture of inhumanity in Iraq. Saddam himself embodied the Humanitarian Theory of Punishment and he should be held to account. What better statement can we offer to those who have spent most of their lives under his jackboot brutality that as a man, he is responsible for his crimes? What better testament can we offer to international justice than to demonstrate to the people of Iraq that the untold misery and death of Saddam's victims demands his life be forfeit for his actions? To do anything less than hang Saddam Hussein is to engage in double-speak and to undermine the very principles of human rights we were told that we invaded Iraq to instill.

It is interesting to note that those complaining about Saddam's death sentence do so in the safety knowing that they will probably never have to live in the culture he helped create, nor will they ever have Saddam Hussein as a neighbor. If Saddam were allowed to live, Iraqis who suffered under his regime would not have those same assurances. Many of those critics are saying that the death of Saddam Hussein will not serve as a deterrent to other tyrants. But making deterrence, rather than desert, the basis of justice is to revert to the Humanitarian Theory of Punishment. What we can assure the Iraqi people of on the day when Saddam dances at the end of a rope is that he will be deterred forever from ever resuming his reign of terror.

May God have mercy on his soul.

Studies Cannot "Prove" Capital Punishment Deters Crime

Clive Stafford Smith

Clive Stafford Smith is legal director of Reprieve, a United Kingdom charity fighting for people facing the death penalty.

Profound moral arguments are rarely resolved by statistical proof, and when an academic claims to have done just that I cannot help but raise a sceptical eyebrow. So you can imagine my reaction earlier this year [2005] when Cass Sunstein and Adrian Vermeule, two law professors at the University of Chicago, published a paper in which they claimed that the death penalty was "morally obligatory" because it had been proved statistically that it deterred people from committing murder. Each execution, they said, saves 18 lives, so "a refusal to impose the death penalty condemns numerous innocent people to death."

Clients Are Not Statistics

I have spent more than 20 years representing some 300 men, women and children who faced capital punishment in various US states. I do not think of my clients as statistics. Six of them have died in the execution chamber. Often I have staved off executions only at the last minute. Many of my clients have been innocent: human beings make fallible judges, and no machine has more human parts than the criminal justice system.

I therefore feel strongly that when academics step out of the classroom and into public discourse on this matter they

Clive Stafford Smith, "Forget the Statistics: Killing Is Wrong," *New Scientist*, vol. 187, August 20, 2005, pp. 20–21. www.newscientist.com. Copyright © 2005 Reed Elsevier Business Publishing, Ltd. Reproduced by permission.

must be held responsible for their actions. And as it turns out, Sunstein and Vermeule should have been a lot more careful before they dished out their verdict.

So let's get this straight: because homicidal maniacs kill people by mistake, . . . then it's supposed to be OK for the state to emulate them.

For a start, they offer nothing in the way of original research. Their paper, "Is Capital Punishment Morally Required?" is a philosophical polemic based on the conclusions of other authors. What's more, the "wave of recent evidence" suggesting that capital punishment saves lives is little more than a ripple. They base their argument on a 2003 paper by Hashem Dezhbakhsh and others, citing it as evidence that each execution saves 18 lives. However, they go on to refer to another study that "proves" each execution saves 14 lives; another proves that only five lives are saved; yet another claims three are saved. Which researchers are we to believe? How would it look if, rather than dealing with life or death, these were financial analysts all promising a profit on an investment but unable to decide whether it would be 3 per cent or 18 per cent? My bet is that you would get nervous about investing.

Deterrence Is Not the Only Issue

Still, is deterrence the only issue at hand when considering the morality of the death penalty? Sunstein and Vermeule seem to think so. They argue that the familiar problems with capital punishment—the danger of executing an innocent person, the "irreversibility" of the sentence, the somewhat arbitrary way it is applied, and the fact that it applies to a disproportionate number of African-Americans—do not add up to a valid case against it because the same distortions occur even more acutely with homicide, which capital punishment can help prevent. So let's get this straight: because homicidal maniacs kill people by mistake, kill them irreversibly, kill them arbitrarily or kill proportionately more African-Americans than whites, then its supposed to be OK for the state to emulate them.

This is untenable, and immoral. My African-American, juvenile, mentally disabled client Ryan Matthews was recently exonerated from death row by six DNA tests. He has only one life, and it would have been no consolation to him, had he been executed in error, that some academic pondering the view from his office window thought that his arbitrary death was OK because the murder for which he was falsely convicted was arbitrary too.

Statistics Are Not the Answer

The crux of my argument is this: the notion that statistics can solve all the world's problems is facile.

Sunstein and Vermeule even hint at the absurdity of their "moral obligation" thesis when they apply it to highway safety. In effect, they argue that if it were proved that a speed limit of 8 kilometers per hour would save 50,000 lives a year on American roads, the government would be morally obligated to impose it—no matter that the average daily commute would take a full 6 hours each way. What saddens me most about this paper is that Sunstein worked as a clerk for a hero of mine, [lawyer and Supreme Court Justice] Thurgood Marshall, who ventured courageously into the South during the dangerous times of the 1950s and early 1960s to defend victims of racial discrimination.

If Sunstein had had the same "real world" experience as Marshall, he might see that there are more sensible approaches than capital punishment to the US's murder epidemic, such as controlling guns. It seems to have worked in Europe. The death penalty is disgusting. I have been there. I have watched my clients die. And I will spend the rest of my life doing my

best to make sure it does not happen to individual human beings who I have come to know.

Capital Punishment Is Ineffective and Dangerous

Michael Cohen

Michael Cohen is professor emeritus of English at Murray State University in Kentucky.

During the point in the jury selection process called *voir dire*, prosecutors and defense attorneys question prospective jurors and, everyone hopes, have their questions answered truthfully. This provides an opportunity for both sides to size up those who will decide the case. The following are the questions I heard while waiting to learn whether I would be empanelled on a jury in a recent capital murder case before the Sixth U.S. District Court (I wasn't selected):

> "Have you or any of those close to you ever been the victim of a violent crime?" *Yes, my father was shot to death when I was a young child.*

> "Do you have any religious or moral beliefs or convictions that would prevent you from imposing a death sentence?" *No.*

> "Do you feel that society has a right to impose the death penalty for especially heinous crimes?" *Yes.*

My answers may puzzle some readers. If I'm not morally opposed to the death penalty—if in fact I would be willing under certain circumstances to impose it—why do I take a position against it?

I oppose the death penalty not because it is morally wrong but because it is ineffective and dangerous. Furthermore, it doesn't deter criminal behavior, it's more expensive than life

Michael Cohen, "The Victims and the Furies in American Courts," *The Humanist*, January–February 2006, pp. 19–23. www.thehumanist.org. Reproduced by permission of the author.

imprisonment, it's unsure, and it's sold politically and implemented widely in ways that pander to racial bigotry. Worst of all, it threatens through another sort of pandering—this time in the name of "victims' rights"—to undermine the very basis of justice.

Vengeance seems to be society's strongest reason for embracing the death penalty.

It is this latter that I wish to discuss in detail.

Revenge Is the Aim of Capital Punishment

Twentieth century journalist and social critic H. L. Mencken pointed out that the shocking or degrading nature of the death penalty is as irrelevant to most people as is the fact that it doesn't deter others from heinous crimes. The most important aim of capital punishment in Mencken's opinion is revenge. The immediate victims of the crime and society as a whole, he says, want "the satisfaction of seeing the criminal actually before them suffer as he made them suffer. What they want is the peace of mind that goes with the feeling that accounts are squared." As usual, Mencken is useful in getting us to admit what really motivates us, regardless of what we claim the justification for our acts might be. Revenge—the ancient spirit embodied for the Greeks in the form of the furies—is the real justification for killing people judicially, and we won't think clearly about the whole process until we admit this to ourselves.

Vengeance seems to be society's strongest reason for embracing the death penalty, regardless of what name we give it. And it doesn't bother most people that it might actually be in conflict with other justifications, such as deterrence. As Gary Wills points out in a June 2001 article in the *New York Review of Books*, juries that impose the death penalty for horrendous crimes "reflect more the anger of society" while they "fail to make the calculations that we are told future murderers will make."

Perhaps the awakening of the furies—this "anger of society," without coolness or reflection—is justified by heinous criminal acts. Perhaps the egregiously cruel, the wantonly violent ([Oklahoma City bomber] Timothy McVeigh once referred to the nineteen young children who died in the Murrah daycare center as "collateral damage"), and the sadistically homicidal acts of murderers justify society's thirst for retribution and reprisal. Never mind that the New Testament revises the so-called biblical injunction of taking an eye for an eye. "When the injury is serious," writes Mencken, "Christianity is adjourned, and even saints reach for their sidearms."

Well, if society is making the judgment on the basis of the wrong done to it as a whole, then it would be futile to cry out against the judgment. But if, as seems more likely, what is increasingly happening is a failure to distinguish between the interests of society and those of the immediate victims, then the whole purpose of a judicial system is being subverted. We need to remind ourselves exactly what justice is and what it replaces, lest we revert to a pattern where vengeance drives all reaction to crime.

Unfortunately, we can't review the origins of law and courts directly because they are lost in prehistory. We can, however, pay attention to what literature and myth tell us about courts of law replacing the rule of revenge.

Law Replaces Vengeance

The *Oresteia* is a group of three plays written by the first great Greek tragic dramatist, Aeschylus, in 458 BCE, when Athens was at the height of its civic and artistic glory. The plays move from a world where violence is answered by violence toward a newer, more civilized world in which Athenian society votes as a jury on guilt and penalties for crimes; law replaces vengeance.

In these plays, Aeschylus gives us a myth about the origin of the justice system, the very system the West later inherited. In the process he shows how society has to absorb and neutralize the force of individual vengeance and the desire for revenge if there is ever to be justice. It's a lesson that has been forgotten in the current furor over victims' rights. We cannot isolate the victims of crimes as somehow being more entitled to retribution; justice means that society as a whole enacts punishment for a crime against society.

The Athenian justice system offers a way out of the cycle of revenge.

In Aeschylus's narrative, which runs through the three plays, the returning Greek king, Agamemnon, is murdered by his wife, Clytemnestra, out of revenge for his sacrifice of their daughter, Iphigenia. Clytemnestra is later killed by their son, Orestes. But when Orestes is pursued by the furies, who wish to avenge his murder of Clytemnestra, Apollo and Athena enter the action to invent the Athenian court system. They try Orestes and eventually acquit him.

The Athenian justice system offers a way out of the cycle of revenge. For Agamemnon and his house—as for any society ruled by blood vengeance—the past has captured the future. Aeschylus expresses this brutal constraint in *Agamemnon*, the first play of the trilogy, with imagery that confounds past, present, and future.

An example comes in the opening, as the old men who make up the chorus recall an event that took place before the Greeks sailed to Troy to avenge the kidnapping of Helen. The priest Calchas, summoned by Agamemnon to figure out why the lack of winds is keeping the avenging Greek fleet from sailing to Troy, reads a sign: two eagles devour the unborn babies of a rabbit. Calchas says the child-protecting goddess Artemis, angered at the coming slaughter of Troy's children, retards the inevitable progress of the Greeks toward their Trojan conquest until the Greek leader serves up his own child as a sacrifice. In the verses of the chorus, the eagles' feast of unborn young is mixed up with the sacrifice of Iphigenia, the slaughter of Trojan Queen Hecuba's children and all the young innocents at Troy, and the outrages that began the curse on Agamemnon's house—namely, the murder and cannibalism of children perpetrated by Agamemnon's father Atreus and his great-grandfather Tantalus.

All of society is implicated and diminished by the killing of one of its members.

Tantalus served his son Pelops to the gods for a meal and was punished by being unable to grasp the grapes he continually reaches for in Hades. Atreus killed the children of his brother Thyestes and then served them to Thyestes for a meal, calling down Thyestes' curse on the family. Agamemnon sacrificed his own child to appease Artemis and eventually was murdered by Clytemnestra in revenge. Orestes, the son of Clytemnestra and Agamemnon, then killed Clytemnestra in revenge for his father. In the imagery of the plays, the present and the future are both controlled by the past. Time is a prison where the deeds of the past are continually recommitted with different victims.

Murder Is a Family Affair

The myth of the cursed house of Atreus illustrates two important truths that must be grasped before any society can achieve even the beginnings of justice. The first truth is that murder is always a family affair in the broadest sense: all of society is implicated and diminished by the killing of one of its members. The Hebrew culture conveys this truth by having the first murder that of brother by brother. But the Greek myth contains another truth not seen in the Genesis tale of Cain and

165

Abel. Though in both stories the first murder is divinely punished and the punishment is continued torment, in the Greek story the human reaction to murder is to answer it with another murder. This mortal vengeance seems a natural response but, as the myth makes clear, it invites further vengeance. The second truth, therefore, is that murder answered by revenge inspires revenge in its turn. To this cycle of retributive vengeance there is no end. In the words of Mohandas Gandhi, "An eye for an eye makes the whole world blind."

Aeschylus' subject is the problem of vengeance and the origin of the justice system to answer it. When Clytemnestra kills Agamemnon she invokes "the three gods to whom I sacrificed this man," which she names as "the child's Rights . . . Ruin . . . and Fury." She also says she is moved by "our savage ancient spirit of revenge." In fact Aeschylus darkens her motivation by having her glory in her adulterous affair with her lover, Aegisthus, and in the power the two of them wield over the city-state of Argos.

Because in Aeschylus' story Clytemnestra's son and killer, Orestes, will eventually escape the cycle of vengeance, the tragedian depicts Orestes not as driven by the furies, the primitive spirits who are the essence of revenge, but as the instrument of Apollo. The god not only threatens Orestes with consequences if he fails to act—ostracism, physical pain, and psychological torture—but he promises his own protection. As Orestes kills his mother offstage, the chorus says that the son is guided by the goddess of justice, Athena, and that "Apollo wills it so!"

Punishment isn't designed to make the victims feel better or experience 'closure.'

Though Orestes is pursued by the furies after he kills his mother, Athena and Apollo arrange it so he is put on trial and acquitted. This requires Apollo to claim that Orestes' act was

Zeus' justice, and the jury comes in at half for conviction and half for acquittal. By breaking the tie and casting her vote for acquittal, Athena symbolically inaugurates the practice that tie votes will result in acquittal. Finally Athena, who knows the furies aren't just going to go away, promises them a place in the depths of the earth and renames them as kindly spirits, the Eumenides.

Though this allegory isn't, itself, an argument against capital punishment or against the belief that a death should be justified with a death, the message is that the wrong done in crime is felt by the whole community. But in this it is felt more impersonally and coolly, objectively and rationally, than how the victims and their immediate families feel it. And when the punishment is removed from the hands of those immediately wronged it is made a less personal matter. The crime is punished rather than the victim avenged. And the punishment isn't designed to make the victims feel better or experience "closure." It is society that is wronged and thus society moves to punish the crime. Until it does so—coolly, not in the heat of vengeance, deliberately rather than swiftly—there will be no justice, only an endless cycle of crime following crime.

Victim Rights Movement

A routine practice in sentencing hearings in U.S. courts these days is the hearing of "impact states"—testimony from the relatives of a murder victim. Their voices cry out because the victims' voices can't. And their emotional pain claims our attention. The burden of those voices is almost always the same: the parents, siblings, and spouses of victims won't achieve peace or, in today's jargon, "find closure," until the murderer is dead and as absent from his or her family as is the victim. Victims' rights organizations have sprung up all over the country, loudly complaining that the courts protect the rights of the accused and even the convicted at the cost of those of victims and the families of victims. It is hardly possible to exaggerate how important and widespread the victims' rights movement has become. According to Scott Turow, whose experience as a member of Illinois Governor Jim Ryan's task force to reform the state's capital punishment system changed him from an advocate to an opponent of the death penalty, "The national victims' rights movement is so powerful that victims have become virtual proprietors of the capital system."

We need to tell victims that revenge is not one of their rights.

It hasn't always been thus. Within the last fifteen years the U.S. Supreme Court reversed its earlier decisions that argued that victims and their families had no role in the process of deciding guilt and passing sentence. As recently as 1987 the Court said that statements by victims and relatives weren't constitutionally admissible at a capital sentencing proceeding. . . .

Society Should Decide Punishment

Aeschylus's fable points us to the real relation that ought to exist between society and victim. We need to tell victims that revenge is *not* one of their rights. In the rule of law, society steps back at least a couple of paces from the victim's position. Society doesn't say to the victim, "Go and take revenge yourself." Neither does society say, "You have been wronged and we will act as your substitute in exacting revenge." Under the law, society measures the extent of harm done to it—to the whole body of the people—and imposes punishment based on that wrong. This degree of abstraction is precisely the measure of your safety and mine from reversion to the rule of the furies.

Abstraction, of course, makes an unsatisfactory meal for victims. My family choked on the verdict of manslaughter rather than murder that enabled my father's killer to get out of prison after merely a year. For victims, a life is "worth" a life, which means taking one demands taking another. The furies, too, argued at the Athenian court that their rule—older than the law, older than the gods—demanded a life for a life, and if their rule weren't honored, they further warned, the center wouldn't hold.

Society has always felt that killings in some circumstances weigh less than they do in others. When it comes to prescribing punishment to the perpetrator, a life taken after its owner puts him- or herself in harm's way—starting a bar fight, for example—doesn't carry the same judicial weight as an innocent life wantonly taken. These are simple, hard facts of society's judgments. A classic case is the crime of passion. The irate husband who kills the adulterer isn't treated in the same way as the serial killer. But if we succumb to the appeal of victims' rights, we can no longer justify the distinction.

A Father Murdered

The widow and the three children of the adulterer—I am one of those three, for this is my father's killing we are looking at here, not an abstract example—suffer his loss as acutely as any mother of one of [serial killer] Jeffrey Dahmer's victims suffers the death of her boy, or any husband or wife of a spouse blown up by Timothy McVeigh. Turow, looking at the issue from a lawyer's point of view, points out that "it violates the fundamental notion that like crimes be punished alike to allow life or death to hinge on the emotional needs of the survivors."

It isn't the business of juries to feel the victims' pain but to decide what harm has been done to society.

The sudden absence of the murder victim from the lives of family and friends means that no one can say "I love you" one more time or make up a quarrel or, in my mother's case, ask, "Why did you betray me?" The anger and perhaps guilt that goes with these cruelly truncated relations generates its own desire for revenge.

But not in my case: I am free from the anger and the guilt. When I think about what should have happened to the man who killed my father, I have a luxury other victims lack: I am emotionally insulated from the event of my father's killing because it happened when I was too young to know what was going on. Such emotional insulation is precisely what society has and needs in order to pursue justice. It isn't the business of juries to feel the victims' pain but to decide what harm has been done to society. It isn't their business to give satisfaction or closure to victims but, rather, to render swift, reliable, unbiased punishment for the harm done to society as a whole. As a victim, I would like juries and the society from which they are chosen to think not as victims do but as members of a responsible body that measures wrong by a different yardstick from emotional pain.

And, as an added benefit, taking the heat of revenge out of the sentencing process means that sentences will be fairer across lines of gender, race, and class because bias is more likely to sneak into the process the more passionately it is conducted. Therefore, we need to restore to our courts the social objectivity the Greeks attained, after so many generations of murder and revenge.

Deterrence Studies Are Inconsistent and Unscientific

Jeffrey Fagan

Jeffrey Fagan is professor of law and public health at Columbia University in New York City.

Chairman [Sam] Brownback, Senator [Russ] Feingold, and Honorable members of the Subcommittee, thank you for inviting me to testify before you today on this most urgent topic. This is an important moment historically in the debate on capital punishment, both in the states and the nation. New developments in social science and law have rekindled the debate on the effectiveness of the death penalty as a deterrent to murder. Both legal scholars and social scientists have transformed this new social science evidence into calls for more executions that they claim will save lives. Others challenge the scientific credibility of these new studies, and warn about the moral hazards and practical risks of capital punishment. Thus, public policy choices on capital punishment may depend on the accuracy, reliability and certainty of this new social science evidence. I appear today to discuss significant errors and flaws that seriously undermine the new social science claims about deterrence, and render moot calls for a vigorous new application of the death penalty. The risks of error in capital punishment, the suspect evidence of its effectiveness as a deterrent, and its high costs that foreclose local investments in basic state and local services, are critical dimensions of public policy choices facing the states and the nation on how to punish those who commit the worst crimes. . . .

Jeffrey Fagan, "Deterrence and the Death Penalty: Risk, Uncertainty, and Public Policy Choices," testimony to the Subcommittee on the Constitution, Civil Rights and Property Rights, Committee on the Judiciary, United States Senate, February 1, 2006. Reproduced by permission of the author.

New Studies Contain Many Errors

Recent studies claiming that executions reduce murders have fueled the revival of deterrence as a rationale to expand the use of capital punishment. Such strong claims are not unusual in either the social or natural sciences, but like nearly all claims of strong causal effects from any social or legal intervention, the claims of a "new deterrence" fall apart under close scrutiny. These new studies are fraught with numerous technical and conceptual errors: inappropriate methods of statistical analysis, failures to consider all the relevant factors that drive murder rates, missing data on key variables in key states, the tyranny of a few outlier states and years, weak to nonexistent tests of concurrent effects of incarceration, statistical confounding of murder rates with death sentences, failure to consider the general performance of the criminal justice system, artifactual results from truncated time frames, and the absence of any direct test of deterrence. These studies fail to reach the demanding standards of social science to make such strong claims, standards such as replication, responding to counterfactual claims, and basic comparisons with other causal scenarios. Social scientists have failed to replicate several of these studies, and in some cases have produced contradictory results with the same data, suggesting that the original findings are unstable, unreliable and perhaps inaccurate. This evidence, together with some simple examples and contrasts including the experience in my state of New York, suggest extreme caution before concluding that there is new evidence that the death penalty deters murders.

The costs of capital punishment are extremely high. Even in states where prosecutors infrequently seek the death penalty, costs of obtaining convictions and executions in capital cases range from $2.5 to $5 million dollars per case (in current dollars), compared to less than $1 million for each killer sentenced to life without parole. Local governments bear the burden of these costs, diverting $2 million per capital trial from local services—hospitals and health care, police and public safety, and education—or infrastructure repairs—roads and other capital expenditures—and causing counties to borrow money or raise local taxes. The costs are often transferred to state governments as "risk pools" or programs of local assistance to prosecute death penalty cases, diffusing death penalty costs to counties that choose not to use—or have no need for—the death penalty in capital cases.

Capital Cases Are Not Cost Effective

The high costs of the death penalty, the unreliable evidence of its deterrent effects, and the fact that the states that execute the most people also have the highest error rates, create clear public policy choices for the nation. If a state is going to spend $500 million on law enforcement over the next two decades, is the *best* use of that money to buy two or three executions or, for example, to fund additional police detectives, prosecutors, and judges to arrest and incarcerate murderers and other criminals who currently escape any punishment because of insufficient law-enforcement resources? Also, most states rarely use the death penalty, and both death sentences and executions have declined sharply over the past five years, even as murder rates have declined nationally. We cannot expect the rare use of the death penalty to have a deterrent effect on already declining rates of murder. [Supreme Court] Justice [Byron R.] White noted long ago in *Furman v. Georgia* that when only a tiny proportion of the individuals who commit murder are executed, the penalty is unconstitutionally irrational: a death penalty that is almost never used serves no deterrent function, because no would-be murderer can expect to be executed. Accordingly, a threshold question for state legislatures across the country is whether their necessary and admirable efforts to avoid error and the horror of the execution of the innocent won't—after many hundreds of millions of dollars of trying—burden the state with a death penalty that will be overturned again because of this additional constitutional problem?

CHAPTER 4

Should Capital Punishment Be Abolished or Reformed?

Chapter Preface

Among the major nations in the Western world, the United States is the only one that sanctions the use of the death penalty. After the U.S. Supreme Court placed a moratorium on the death penalty in 1972, the court reinstated the practice five years later, in 1977. Although critics of the death penalty take some comfort in the fact that the practice is waning in this country, they realize that there is no groundswell to abolish it. Nevertheless, many supporters of the death penalty fear that the Supreme Court could rule capital punishment unconstitutional again if the United Nations (UN) adopts a resolution to abolish it worldwide.

In 1948 the UN first sought to abolish the death penalty with the adoption of the Universal Declaration of Human Rights. Article 3 states, "everyone has the right to life, liberty and security of person." It is important to note that a declaration, unlike a convention or covenant, is not a binding treaty. With this in mind, in 1966 the UN adopted the International Covenant on Civil and Political Rights. This legal instrument encourages UN member states to abolish the death penalty. Article 6 reads, "every human being has the inherent right to life. This right shall be protected by law. No one shall be arbitrarily deprived of his life." However, Article 7 states, "sentence of death may be imposed only for the most serious crime . . . pursuant to a final judgment rendered by a competent court." Therefore, signatory countries that sanction the death penalty are permitted to retain it.

In March 2007, following the execution of Saddam Hussein, the UN General Assembly stepped up its effort to pressure the United States to put an end to the death penalty. Louise Arbour, the UN's high commissioner for human rights, said,

> There is a renewed momentum, or focus, or interest on the question of the abolition of the death penalty. It's been possibly fueled by the concerns, or the visibility of the executions in Iraq, which, in a sense, I think mobilised international public attention on the question of the death penalty and I would certainly hope that in the course of this year, we will see renewed efforts, debate, discussion on that issue.

The following month, Italy began petitioning the general assembly to adopt a resolution calling for an immediate and universal moratorium on death sentences and executions and the commutation of existing death sentences, with a view to the universal abolition of the death penalty. This resolution would nullify Article 7 of the International Covenant on Civil and Political Rights, which recognizes the rulings of sovereign courts.

Joseph A. Klein, the author of *Global Deception: The UN's Stealth Assault on America's Freedom* (2005), argues that if adopted, the Italian resolution could have undue influence on the U.S. Supreme Court. He argues that a majority of Supreme Court justices are increasingly looking to model prevailing "standards of decency" after those of the international community. He fears that American legal precedents will no longer matter because the Supreme Court will ultimately agree with the UN that the death penalty is inherently a cruel and unusual punishment that should be repealed. The UN is also aware of this possibility. Recently, High Commissioner Arbour commented,

> If the courts are willing to listen to us, we are not going to shy away. It depends on our own capacity to make a contribution in a case where the advocacy of international standards are not likely to be advanced by others.

The Italian resolution has eighty-eight member state supporters. At least one hundred signatures, however, are required for supporters to be confident that a moratorium could win a majority vote in the 192-member general assembly.

Executions Should Be Televised to Spur Debate About Capital Punishment

Howard Rosenberg

Howard Rosenberg is a Pulitzer Prize–winning TV columnist for the Los Angeles Times.

I want to see Scott Peterson die.

Don't misunderstand: I don't want him dead, despite his conviction for the murder of his wife, Laci, and their unborn son. Too many innocent souls have landed on Death Row through the years for me to endorse capital punishment.

Not everyone shares my disdain for the death penalty. It's on the books in 38 states, and 66% of Americans still give it the thumbs up, according to Gallup polls.

Regardless, body counts shouldn't be abstractions, flicked away like lint and banished to the subconscious. That's true for Iraq, where deaths of U.S. troops, innocent civilians and others are rising while the Pentagon, largely with media acquiescence, resists exposing these bodies to public view, as if Americans should not witness the human cost of a war most of them support.

Televise Executions

And it's true for executions.

So televise them. I want to see for myself, not just hear from others, what it's like when government ends a life. *That* would be a reality show.

Howard Rosenberg, "Kill Him on TV," *Broadcasting & Cable*, December 20, 2004, p. 30. Reproduced by permission.

Details would have to be worked out, but try this:

Executions would be videotaped and telecast late at night, beyond normal viewing hours of young children. They would be tightly structured. Attention would be given to the crimes and victims and their loved ones, with no softening of pain. There would be no glorifying eulogies or metaphorical walks into a sunset for doomed inmates. Each condemned person would have limited time for final remarks. And if there were expletives, not to worry, FCC; they'd be bleeped.

Executions would be videotaped and telecast late at night, beyond normal viewing hours of young children.

Peterson's death penalty must still be formalized by the judge in the case. Moreover, the appeals process should keep him on California's Death Row for years.

If he is executed, watching won't be pleasant. I can take it, though, and you can, too. We're veterans of death on TV, after all, from Jack Ruby gunning down Lee Harvey Oswald in 1963 to an armed motorist blowing away half his face on a Los Angeles freeway in 1998. As Matt Roush noted in this magazine recently, TV crime dramas now serve a "forensic feast of splatter analysis and body-cavity voyeurism."

If the TV lens is our designated peeper—from fictional *CSI* to gratuitous "gotcha" footage on newscasts—then have it count for something beyond frivolous diversion.

Public Executions Could Change Minds

Would televising executions change minds? Possibly. How much sooner, for example, would Florida have switched to lethal injections, as it did in 2000, if its electric chair, nicknamed "Old Sparky," had been shown torching men like Roman candles as it killed them?

Televising executions might even completely turn around death-penalty advocates, although just as likely it would desensitize them to the process.

In any case, enlightenment, not grisly titillation, would be the goal. At last, Americans would gain visual access to public policy whose full extent reaches them now only through the thick filters of Hollywood and a handful of reporters designated as eyewitnesses. Sean Penn was chillingly persuasive when meeting the big needle in *Dead Man Walking*, observed by Susan Sarandon as his pious pen pal. But actual executions aren't scenes that end with "Cut!"

If [Timothy] McVeigh's execution was fit for viewing for them [surviving victims and family members], why not for the rest of us?

Democracies are meant to operate in the open. If there is nothing to hide, if Americans truly dislike government in shadows, they shouldn't oppose TV cameras inside state killing rooms. Nor, for the same reason, should pro-choicers resist telecasts of legal abortions.

It's true that we sanction many things without desiring to witness them. We approve surgery, for one, but are too queasy to watch it. Also, meat eaters haven't the stomach to peek inside a slaughterhouse, even through a TV lens.

The difference is that government doesn't ban cameras from these venues, which *are* televised on occasion. Government does ban cameras from executions.

Dead issue walking? I hope not.

The McVeigh Execution

Televised executions were my crusade long before 2001, when Attorney General John Ashcroft made an exception and approved the closed-circuit telecast of Oklahoma City bomber Timothy McVeigh's death by lethal injection in Terre Haute,

Ind. He did so to accommodate nearly 300 surviving victims and family members who wanted to watch.

I applauded Ashcroft, thinking that seeing McVeigh die might bring those folks peace or closure. But when I requested a seat myself at the closed-circuit telecast, the U.S. Bureau of Prisons rejected me because I wasn't a bombing survivor or victim's relative.

If McVeigh's execution was fit viewing for them, why not for the rest of us? If they had earned this opportunity, why hadn't all Americans, many of whom also bore emotional scars from the bombing?

In 1998, since-imprisoned Dr. Jack Kevorkian was shown giving a lethal injection to someone with advanced Lou Gehrig's disease in a *60 Minutes* segment that tackled mercy killing. Similarly, televising executions would sharpen dialogue about the death penalty, in the news increasingly now because of the potential of enhanced DNA to either affirm or disprove guilt.

This would not foster a return to an earlier age of public hangings and beheadings, when executions were viewed as family entertainment.

Would televised executions be tasteless, though? I imagine—just as they are when occurring beyond public view.

Capital Punishment Is a Failed Experiment and Should Be Abolished

Anna Quindlen

Anna Quindlen is a prize-winning journalist, best-selling novelist, and contributing editor at Newsweek.

You brush up against a lot of weird stuff in the course of child rearing, but one phenomenon that always had me scratching my head was the parents who hit their kids to teach them that hitting was a bad thing.

In their defense, they had a civic model for that kind of bizarre circular reasoning. Americans still live in one of the few countries that kill people to make clear what a terrible thing killing people is.

Hardly any other civilized place does this anymore. In the past three decades, the number of nations that have abolished the death penalty has risen from 16 to 86. Last year [in 2005] four countries accounted for nearly all executions worldwide: China, Iran, Saudi Arabia and the United States.

As my Irish grandmother used to say, you're known by the company you keep.

Last week the Supreme Court agreed to cogitate once more about capital punishment, a boomerang the justices find coming back at them time and time again. This new case is about the way lethal injection is administered. The argument is that even though one drug anesthetizes, a second paralyzes and a third stops the heart, the first is not sufficient to mitigate the pain and the second makes the inmate appear peaceful when he is in agony.

In other words, the case is about whether being put to death hurts. Passing judgment on this particular issue is the equivalent of diagramming an ungrammatical sentence.

Much of the debate about the death penalty since it reared its ugly head again in the '70s has been about whether it is disproportionately meted out to poor minorities, whether it should be permitted for juvenile offenders, whether various methods constitute cruel and unusual punishment. Most of these discussions are designed not to examine underlying deep moral issues but to allow Americans to continue to put people to death and still feel good about themselves.

Since 1976, more than a thousand men and women have been executed in the United States.

That's become increasingly difficult. At the same time the court decided to revisit lethal injection, the justices agreed to a federal hearing in the case of a man who has spent 20 years on death row. He was convicted of raping and murdering a neighbor. The prosecution said his semen was found on the dead woman. New DNA tests show that the semen was instead that of her husband, who witnesses say had drunkenly confessed to the murder.

This is just one of a long line of such cases. Accusers recant, guilty parties confess, the lab makes a match that wasn't possible before. Since 1976, more than a thousand men and women have been executed in the United States. But during that same period more than 123 death-row inmates have been exonerated. That's a terrible statistical average. Put another way, more than 123 individuals truly guilty of savage crimes were walking free while someone else sat waiting on death row. And most, if not all, of those death-row inmates would have been wrongly executed if not for the lengthy appeals process death-penalty advocates like to decry.

Some years ago the execution of a woman named Karla Faye Tucker in Texas got a lot of attention. She had been found guilty of a particularly heinous double murder involving a pickax. But in jail she had a religious conversion so transformative that she referred to the place where she was held as "life row."

This is one of those issues where there isn't really a middle ground.

When Tucker was put to death, there was a mob scene outside the prison. Some of those who gathered there were opponents of the death penalty. Some wanted the execution to proceed. And some of the latter group danced and laughed and cheered and acted as though they were at the Super Bowl and their team had just scored a touchdown. They did everything but sell funnel cakes. If they had lived 300 years earlier, they would have happily paraded through cobbled streets with Karla Faye's head on a pike.

Most people who support capital punishment can't be counted as members of that sorry fringe mob. But this is one of those issues where there isn't really a middle ground. Just because the electric chair has been phased out doesn't mean civilization has prevailed; it only means that people didn't like how reports of a convicted man's head bursting into flame made them feel about what they were doing. In judicial terms, Justice Harry Blackmun concluded in 1994 that all it came down to was figuring out how to "tinker with the machinery of death."

And he was officially finished with it, writing: "Rather than continue to coddle the Court's delusion that the desired level of fairness has been achieved and the need for regulation eviscerated, I feel morally and intellectually obligated simply to concede that the death penalty experiment has failed." The question isn't whether executions can be made painless: It's whether they're wrong. Everything else is just quibbling. And most of the quibbling simply boils down to trying to make the wrong seem right.

Feminists Should Advocate to Abolish Capital Punishment

Laura Huey

Laura Huey is an assistant professor of sociology at Concordia University in Montreal, Canada.

On 11 January 2001, the state of Oklahoma executed Wanda Jean Allen. As a killer—she murdered her former lover in an apparent fit of jealousy and despair—she was unremarkable. As a "regular" citizen of the state before the commission of her crime, she would likely have attracted little public attention—she was poor, black, female, lesbian, and had an IQ that tested in the range of 80. Her execution certainly drew little attention; there was no large public outcry against her death, and none of the media frenzy that attended the execution of Karla Faye Tucker some two years earlier.

In trying to understand Allen's death, and the public's reaction to this event, or, more appropriately, lack of reaction, I have been questioning the roles that race, gender, socioeconomic status, and sexuality played in how we—the general public—understood and accepted this event. Undoubtedly, we can trace such connections, and they are worthy of exploration; however, in reflecting upon this event what has struck me most noticeably is less the public's apathy towards understanding Allen's death, and those of similar others enacted through ritualized violence, but the lack of discussion of these events within feminist circles. For example, in reviewing the literature on capital punishment in the US, I could locate very few recent works on the subject by feminist scholars. Of those few that I did find, their content seemed singularly focused on

Laura Huey, "The Abolition of Capital Punishment as a Feminist Issue," *Feminist Review*, vol. 78, no. 1, 2004, pp. 175–180. Reproduced with permission of Palgrave Macmillan.

what is a narrowly framed research question: "to what extent do gender constructs play a role in the receipt and/or execution of a death sentence."

Feminists Must Abort Capital Punishment

In short, of late, we feminists don't seem to want to talk about capital punishment or its abolition. Thus, my purpose here is to respond to what is both present and absent in the feminist literature on the death penalty in order to open a much-needed discussion of this subject among feminist scholars, researchers and activists. In doing so, I am posing a question to you, the reader: "is the abolition of capital punishment a feminist issue?" As I argue throughout, to the extent that the death penalty clearly offends the values and goals that we hold dear, this is a question that can only be answered in the affirmative.

No Western state has recognized anything less than a fully born individual as a citizen *of a state.*

One possible explanation for our relative silence on the subject of capital punishment can be found in [American writer B.] Cruikshank's discussion of the gendered politics that took place surrounding the execution of Karla Faye Tucker. Cruikshank offers the following reason for her own abstention from taking a public stand on abolition: "Much as I would like to be able to persuade the reader that capital punishment is wrong, any moral or humanist argument that I might make about the value of life is pointless in the present context, in which a substantial majority is calling for blood." For Cruikshank, capital punishment serves as a battleground upon which strategic contests are played out. Thus appeals in support of abolition, her own included, would serve no larger purpose, or produce any other effect than to become more rhetoric slung in battle. This is an understandable, albeit unfortunate and ultimately untenable position to take. All social issues by their very nature are contests. In this, capital punishment is no different from women's fights over reproductive rights. Both are said to be in the public interest, but each involve struggles for the control of individual bodies. However, I suspect that few feminists would advance the argument that we ought not to take a stand on reproductive rights because we might not be effective. Similarly, the fact that abolition is a minority position in the US ought not have an influence on whether we adopt it as a feminist issue—I recall that not long ago the holding of feminist principles placed one in a minority.

Abortion and Death Penalty Are Not Analogous

I have raised here what might seem to be a controversial analogy: the struggle against capital punishment as akin to the struggle for reproductive rights. It is potentially controversial because of the "pro-life" contention that these two phenomena are morally equivalent. This point is similarly raised by [American writer] Camille Paglia who argues that "the same people who opposed capital punishment ironically fought for abortion on demand, showing a peculiar discrimination about whom to execute." Given the continuing struggles to ensure our reproductive rights, the moral equivalency proposition provides one very logical reason as to why some feminists may avoid public discussions of capital punishment as a feminist concern. However, contrary to what Paglia, and the "pro-life" contingent suggest, the two issues—capital punishment and reproductive rights—are only analogous with respect to a women's right of privacy and personal autonomy. They are not analogous with respect to the nature of the activities involved; the former involves taking the life of an individual who is recognized as a *citizen* under law, the latter does not. Rights, such as the right to bodily autonomy and integrity (what Western courts have termed "privacy" and/or "self-determination"), are granted to *citizens*. As of this writing, no Western state has recognized anything less than a fully born individual as a *citizen* of a state.

In relation to this analogy, I want to make one further point. It is sometimes very difficult to view women who have been convicted of committing particularly heinous crimes as being anything but monsters. However, when feminists talk about rights, we don't distinguish between "deserving" and "undeserving" women. We don't talk about limiting rights to only those women who are of a particular colour, socio-economic status, and/or to whom we feel sympathy towards because of their life histories. Further, if we view control over women's bodies as a women's issue, and we are not willing to limit women's self-determination in this regard, then it leads us down a highly problematic (and contradictory) path to allow capital punishment as being acceptable for "some of us"—to distinguish between those of us deemed as "deserving," and others who are not. In order to avoid confusion, I want to be clear: preserving a right to privacy and integrity of one's body does not rule out the exceptional ability of the state to hold that body through lawful incarceration or detention. Nor does it rule out the possibility of some minor infringements of privacy or integrity, subject to legislation or judicial order (i.e. the taking of blood samples). However, it ought to bar the state from making the ultimate decision with respect to a *citizen's* body—the ending of her life.

Execution of Women Could Become Routine

I suppose that it could be argued that the death penalty, being a punishment that disproportionately falls upon men, and in some cases for crimes against women, is not a proper concern for feminists. This argument is, however, based on faulty logic. Implicit in it is a view of feminism that is unjustifiably narrow. It suggests that feminists are only concerned with inequality as it pertains to women, that the operation of sexism, racism, homophobia, as they relate to men singly and in combination, are not our concern. Were that the case, we would be stuck with a rather limited conception of feminism, and one that would hardly bring us closer to fulfilling our goal of true equality. Further, there are women on America's death rows. As of this writing [2004], women awaiting execution number fifty. Since 1976, when the Supreme Court restored the death penalty in *Gregg v. Georgia*, ten women have been executed in the US. Given that in the 26 years following *Gregg* 834 men have also been executed, this number may seem insignificant. There are two responses to this view. First, as [Phyllis] Carroll cogently explains:

> The death penalty is a system of raw power. For political outsiders like women and minorities it carries with it a ripple effect that expands through their whole experience. They walk a boundary that they have no power to draw, or even to know when it will be drawn. In this sense, feminists who claim concern over marginalization cannot afford not to study women on death row. Despite their sparse number, women on death row are powerful prisoners of the state and social expectations of womanhood, and their very existence defines us all.

Second, there is every indication that, despite their overall low numbers on death row, the executions of women will become as depressingly routine as those of men. I note that within a 21-year period—between 1976 and 1997—only one woman, Velma Barfield, was executed. No woman was executed between 1984 and 1998. Then, within a 5-year period from 1998 to December 2002, nine women were executed.

Abolition Is the Only Answer

In an examination of the "chivalry hypothesis"—that gender conforming women receive the benefits of gender discrimination by being sentenced to death less often than men for violent crimes—[writer E.] Rapaport points out that if this hypothesis is correct, the benefits to those women who escape the death penalty are offset by ideological costs to women as a whole that are too high. As she explains,

> The reputed leniency that women receive with respect to death sentencing supports the view widely held in our society that women are incapable of achieving nor are they in fact held to, the same standards of personal responsibility as are men. Although there may well be fields of endeavor in which the most profound forms of equality call for recognition of difference, equal democratic citizenship can proceed from no other premise then that of equal personal responsibility for decisions and actions. The chivalry from which women supposedly benefit is too costly: In ideological coin it is supposed to be repaid with tacit recognition of the moral inferiority of females and our lack of aptitude for full citizenship. As a matter of both logic and political necessity, then, feminists must embrace either gender-neutral evenhandedness on abolitionism.

We ought to be more concerned when the issues raised involve the deaths of our sisters and brothers, not only in the West, but across the globe.

I would agree with Rapaport's conclusion that abolition would seem to be a logical and political necessity for feminists. However, I find problematic the fact that she holds out the possibility of gender-neutral evenhandedness as a reasonable alternative to abolition. The problem with this traditionally liberal feminist position is that true equality, in both formal and substantive terms, remains a hoped-for goal rather than a present reality. As Rapaport herself affirms, the law is an imperfect institution that remains some distance from being able to guarantee a true measure of equality. Indeed, I note that much of her article is taken up with showing how gender discrimination is built into the laws, resulting in women receiving death sentences for intimate killings (including in cases where credible allegations of domestic violence have been raised), and men receiving death sentences for stranger killings—creating yet another legal double-standard. Pinning our hopes on a possible happy ending/new beginning does little to address the very real situation of women and men on death row today. Thus, for feminists committed to an egalitarian struggle, abolition remains the only viable answer.

Feminists Should Be Outraged

To conclude, I believe that feminist thought can provide a compelling critique of the practice of legal homicide. Should it be applied to this end? Yes. Feminists have historically been concerned with the operation of discrimination in relation to gender, and, more recently, as it intersects with issues of "race"/ethnicity, class, sexuality and other marginalized status. Further, feminists have long spoken to a broad range of issues outside of what could narrowly be construed as the concerns of women, including on issues relating to the economy, development, and on the operation of institutions such as the criminal justice system. We have critiqued, fought against, and offered alternatives, to policies, practices and institutions that are seen to foster inequality and its pernicious effects, towards the goal of creating an equality-based society. As feminists, then, we are concerned about equality in the administration of justice, and we *ought* to be more concerned when the issues raised involve the deaths of our sisters and brothers, not only in the West, but across the globe. This concern should increase further still—indeed, turn to an outrage that moves us—where we have a substantial body of evidence to the effect that sentences of death have been, and continue to be, handed down in clearly arbitrary and discriminatory ways.

Saddam Hussein Should Not Have Been Hanged

Richard Dawkins

Richard Dawkins is an evolutionary biologist at Oxford University in England.

The obvious objections to the execution of Saddam Hussein are valid and well aired. His death will provoke violent strife between Sunni and Shiite Muslims, and between Iraqis in general and the American occupation forces. This was an opportunity to set a good example of civilized behavior in dealing with a barbarically uncivilized man. In any case, revenge is an ignoble motive. If President [George W.] Bush and British Prime Minister Tony Blair are eventually put on trial for war crimes, I shall not be among those pressing for them to be hanged.

But I want to add another and less obvious objection: Hussein's mind would have been a unique resource for historical, political and psychological research, a resource that is now forever unavailable to scholars.

Saddam's Execution Was Irresponsible

Imagine that some science-fiction equivalent of Simon Wiesenthal [Nazi death camp survivor who hunted down war criminals] built a time machine, traveled back to 1945 and returned to the present with a manacled Adolf Hitler. What should we do with him? Execute him? No, a thousand times no. Historians squabbling over exactly what happened in the Third Reich and World War II would never forgive us for destroying the central witness to all the inside stories, and one of the pivotal influences on 20th century history. Psychologists, struggling to understand how an individual human being could be so evil and so devastatingly effective at persuading others to join him, would give their eyeteeth for such a rich research subject.

Kill Hitler? You would have to be mad to do so. Yet that is undoubtedly what we would have done if he hadn't killed himself in 1945. Hussein is not in the same league as Hitler, but, nevertheless, in a small way his execution represents a wanton and vandalistic destruction of important research data.

[Those] studying the processes by which unscrupulous leaders arise and take over national institutions, have now lost key evidence forever.

He should have been locked up, by all means. Kept him in jail for the rest of his life, to be sure. But to execute him was irresponsible. Hussein could have provided irreplaceable help to future historians of the Iran-Iraq war, of the invasion of Kuwait and of the subsequent era of sanctions culminating in the invasion. Uniquely privileged evidence on the American government's enthusiastic arming of Hussein in the 1980s is now snuffed out at the tug of a rope (no doubt to the relief of Donald Rumsfeld [secretary of defense from 2001 to 2006] and other guilty parties; it is surely no accident that the trial of Hussein neglected those of his crimes that might—no, would—have implicated them).

Loss of Key Evidence Forever

Political scientists of the future, studying the processes by which unscrupulous leaders arise and take over national institutions, have now lost key evidence forever. But perhaps the most important research in which a living Saddam Hussein could have helped is psychological. Most people can't even come close to understanding how any man could be so cruel as Hitler or Hussein, or how such transparently evil monsters could secure sufficient support to take over an entire country.

What were the formative influences on these men? Was it something in their childhood that turned them bad? In their genes? In their testosterone levels? Could the danger have been nipped in the bud by an alert psychiatrist? How would Hitler or Hussein have responded to a different style of education? We don't have a clear answer to these questions. We need to do the research.

Wasn't the judicial destruction of one of the very few research subjects we had . . . an act of vandalism?

Are there lots of Husseins and lots of Hitlers in every society, with most ending up as football hooligans wrecking trains rather than dictators wrecking countries? If so, what singles out the minority that do come to power? Or were men such as these truly unusual? What can we do to prevent them gaining power in the future? Are there changes we could make to our political institutions that would make it harder for men of Hitler's or Hussein's psychological types to take them over?

These questions are not just academically fascinating but potentially of vital importance for our future. And they cannot be answered by prejudice or preconception or intuitive common sense. The only way to answer them is by research. It is in the nature of research on ruthless national dictators that the sample size is small. Wasn't the judicial destruction of one of the very few research subjects we had—and a prime specimen at that—an act of vandalism?

Public and State Support for the Death Penalty Is Declining

Dahlia Lithwick

Dahlia Lithwick covers legal affairs for the online magazine Slate.

In a curious application of Newtonian physics, public and state support for capital punishment is steadily declining in America just as the resolve to maintain the death penalty seems to be hardening in the one arena where death-penalty policy once had seemed poised to change: the Supreme Court.

The trend is clear. According to the Death Penalty Information Center, which compiles statistics on capital punishment, two states have imposed formal moratoriums on the death penalty; executions in New York are on hold after the state's death penalty law was declared unconstitutional in 2004; 11 states (including, most recently, Florida and Tennessee) have effectively barred the practice because of concerns over lethal injection; and 11 more are considering moratoriums or repeals.

The raw numbers of executions and death sentences in the United States have plummeted: Information Center statistics show that in 1999 we executed 98 people, and in 2006 that number dropped to a 10-year low of 53. Whereas America steadily condemned about 300 prisoners a year to death through the 1990s, that number has declined by more than half and reached a low of 114 in 2006. Public support also seems to be faltering. A Gallup poll last year showed that two-thirds of the country still supports capital punishment for murderers, but when given the choice between the death penalty and a life sentence without parole, more people preferred the life prison term (48 percent) to capital punishment (47 percent) for the first time in 20 years.

Growing Doubts

The new uncertainty over capital punishment ranges from queasiness over the methods of execution to concern that we are executing innocents. Lethal injection, the preferred method of execution in 39 of the 40 states that permit capital punishment, is particularly fraught with problems.

In December, then-Gov. Jeb Bush of Florida ended executions following one in which it took the prisoner 34 minutes to die and he suffered chemical burns in the process. Recent scholarship, including a British medical journal report, indicates that the lethal-injection cocktail used may simply mask agonizing pain before death. And state courts are also increasingly bothered about the proper role of physicians—often mandated by law to supervise the lethal-injection process over objections by medical associations and ethics boards.

There are numerous other reasons for our growing doubts about the death penalty. In a 2005 speech, [Supreme Court] Justice John Paul Stevens pointed to several, including DNA evidence that has shown that "a substantial number of death sentences have been imposed erroneously," the fact that elected judges face disproportionate pressure to impose capital punishment, and the problem of "death-qualified" jurors (those who oppose capital punishment are barred from sitting on capital cases). For these and other reasons, many Americans have begun to worry that the death penalty in this country is not reserved for the "worst of the worst," but for the poorest of the poor and those whose trial attorneys later prove to have been asleepest at the switch.

The Innocence Project, a nonprofit legal clinic associated with the Benjamin N. Cardozo School of Law at Yeshiva University in New York, says there have been 194 post-conviction DNA exonerations. A wrongful-executions study by Hugo Bedau and Michael Radelet contends that from 1900 to 1991, 416 clearly innocent people were sentenced to die. And studies about the racism that taints the entire system are unequivocal.

The Supreme Court May Not Have Doubts

In recent years the Supreme Court has also shown concern about the death penalty. In an article published last year, Duke University professor Erwin Chemerinsky observed that in the final years of the William H. Rehnquist Court, the justices showed a marked tendency to overturn death sentences. Chemerinsky speculated that "a majority of the Court was (and continues to be) deeply concerned about how the death penalty is administered in the United States" and that, as a result of the revelations by various investigators, "the reality of innocent people facing execution has had a profound effect on the Justices."

There is some reason to fear that some justices don't share the burgeoning sense that the machinery of death in this country is broken.

So in the early years of the new century, the court handed down surprising decisions outlawing executions of the mentally retarded and of those who were juveniles at the time of their crimes, and refining the tests for the ineffectiveness of counsel. Several justices also voiced concerns off the bench: Stevens, Ruth Bader Ginsburg and Sandra Day O'Connor each spoke publicly and passionately about flaws in the capital system.

But, largely as a result of a change in the court's composition, that trend may now be ending. Just as a few states are defiantly expanding their use of the death penalty. And there is some reason to fear that some justices don't share the burgeoning sense that the machinery of death in this country is broken. One is the new chief justice, John G. Roberts Jr., who, when he worked in the Reagan White House, wrote a memo suggesting that the high court could cut its caseload by "abdicating the role of fourth or fifth guesser in death penalty cases."

One case last term involved a man convicted of a rape and murder, who later produced DNA evidence raising serious doubt that he was the culprit. The court ruled 5 to 3 that this new evidence warranted a new hearing. But Roberts led the dissenters, who felt it wasn't enough for the new evidence to cast doubt on the defendant's conviction; to grant relief, the evidence had to prove he "was actually innocent."

In another death-penalty case from 2005, then-Justice O'Connor agreed with the court's liberals that trial counsel was ineffective. That decision reversed an opinion by Samuel A. Alito Jr., then a judge on the U.S. Court of Appeals for the 3rd Circuit, that would have denied relief. The signals are still mixed. In a different case, the entire court allowed death-row inmates to pursue a civil claim against lethal injection.

If the death penalty in this country needs fixing, the state legislatures should do it.

The Culture War Continues

But also last term, Justice Antonin Scalia wrote a separate opinion in a death-penalty case for the sole purpose of excoriating Justice David H. Souter, who had written in a dissent about exonerated innocents. Scalia's opinion was a full-bore attack on the notion of innocent exonerees "paraded by various professors" and claimed, in effect, that even if those exonerated were not guilty enough to warrant the death penalty, they were still far from "innocent." (How that made them candidates for the death penalty he did not explain.)

Oral argument this term has also revealed a subtle hardening on the part of some of the court's conservatives. In one case, Roberts questioned the need for a trial judge to specifically guide jurors regarding mitigating evidence.

Somehow, just as the American people are beginning to consider the grave injustices pervading the capital system, several justices seem to be staking out strong personal positions on this front in the culture wars.

In his article, Chemerinsky suggests that justices who change course on the death penalty often do so only after decades on the bench. That might suggest that the two new justices will only soften on capital punishment in the far distant future. These justices also would insist that if the death penalty in this country needs fixing, the state legislatures should do it, a process that's already beginning to happen. But if for most Americans the time for stubborn certainty about the death penalty, at least as it's currently practiced, seems to be over, a court that is more certain than ever of its fundamental fairness looks grievously out of step with an American public willing to recognize the dangers of injustice, error and doubt.

Organizations to Contact

The editors have compiled the following list of organizations concerned with the issues debated in this book. The descriptions are derived from materials provided by the organizations. All have publications or information available for interested readers. The list was compiled when the present volume was published; the information provided here may have changed since then. Be aware that many organizations take several weeks or longer to respond to inquiries, so allow as much time as possible.

American Bar Association Death Penalty Moratorium Implementation Project
740 Fifteenth Street NW, Washington, DC   20005
(202) 662-1000
e-mail: moratorium@abanet.org
Web site: www.abanet.org/moratorium/welcome.html

The Death Penalty Moratorium Implementation Project was launched in September 2001 as the American Bar Association's "next step" in working to obtain a nationwide moratorium on executions. The project was created to encourage other bar associations to press for moratoriums in their jurisdictions and to encourage state government leaders to establish moratoriums and undertake detailed examinations of capital punishment laws and processes in their jurisdictions. The project issues assessment reports and background information on the death penalty in several states.

American Civil Liberties Union (ACLU)
125 Broad Street, Nineteenth Floor, New York, NY   10004
(212) 607-3300 • fax: (212) 607-3318
Web site: www.aclu.org

The ACLU, founded in 1920, is a nonprofit organization of more than 500,000 members and supporters. The organization handles nearly 6,000 court cases annually from its offices in almost every state. The mission of the ACLU is to preserve our constitutional rights and to protect segments of the population that have been denied their rights. The organization offers numerous publications on criminal justice, including the *Case Against the Death Penalty*.

Amnesty International

5 Penn Plaza, Fourteenth Floor, New York, NY 10001
(212) 807-8400 • fax: (212) 463-9193
e-mail: www.amnestyusa.org
Web site: www.amnestyusa.org

Amnesty International is a worldwide movement of people who campaign for internationally recognized human rights. Its vision is of a world in which every person enjoys all of the human rights enshrined in the Universal Declaration of Human Rights and other international human rights standards. Each year Amnesty International publishes a report on its work and its concerns throughout the world. It also publishes numerous individual country reports and briefings.

Campaign to End the Death Penalty (CEDP)

National Office, PO Box 25730, Chicago, IL 60625
(773) 955-4841 • fax: (773) 955-4841
e-mail: cedp@nodeathpenalty.org
Web site: http://nodeathpenalty.org

The Campaign to End the Death Penalty (CEDP) is the only national membership-driven, chapter-based grassroots organization dedicated to the abolition of capital punishment in the United States. It works hand in hand with those who have experienced the horrors of death row firsthand—death row inmates themselves and their family members—and works to ensure that their voices are at the forefront of their movement. The group publishes a newsletter called the *Abolitionist* and offers a pamphlet titled *Five Reasons to Oppose the Death Penalty*.

Center for Wrongful Convictions
Northwestern University School of Law, Chicago, IL   60611
(312) 503-2391 • fax: (312) 908-0529
e-mail: cwc@law.northwestern.edu
Web site: www.law.northwestern.edu/depts/clinic/wrongful

The Center for Wrongful Convictions is dedicated to identifying and rectifying wrongful convictions and other serious miscarriages of justice. The center faculty, staff, cooperating outside attorneys, and Northwestern University's Bluhm Legal Clinic students investigate possible wrongful convictions and represent imprisoned clients with claims of actual innocence. The center pioneered the investigation and litigation of wrongful convictions that were a driving force behind both Governor George H. Ryan's decision to suspend executions in Illinois and the current nationwide movement to reform the criminal justice system.

The Constitution Project
1025 Vermont Avenue NW, Third Floor
Washington, DC   20005
(202) 580-6920 • fax: (202) 580-6929
e-mail: info@constitutionproject.org
Web site: www.constitutionproject.org

The Constitution Project seeks consensus solutions to difficult legal and constitutional issues through constructive dialogue across ideological and partisan lines, scholarship, activism, and public education efforts. The Constitution Project has seven active initiatives, each guided by a distinguished bipartisan, blue-ribbon committee. The committee has recently updated its report *Mandatory Justice: The Death Penalty Revisited* (February 2006), taking a look at recent progress and still-needed reforms in capital punishment systems in the United States.

Death Penalty Focus
870 Market Street, Suite 859, San Francisco, CA   94102
(415) 243-0143 • fax: (415) 243-0994

e-mail: information@deathpenalty.org
Web site: www.deathpenalty.org

Death Penalty Focus, founded in 1988, is a nonprofit organization dedicated to the abolition of capital punishment through grassroots organizing, research, and the dissemination of information about the death penalty and its alternatives. It believes that capital punishment is an effective and brutally simplistic response to the serious and complex problem of violent crime. The organization publishes the *Sentry*, a semi-annual newsletter; the *Catalyst*, a monthly e-mail bulletin; *For the Record*, a legislative bulletin; and many informative brochures.

The Death Penalty Information Center (DPIC)
1101 Vermont Avenue NW, Suite 701, Washington, DC   20005
(202) 289-2275 • fax: (202) 289-7336
Web site: www.deathpenaltyinfo.org

The DPIC is a nonprofit organization serving the media and the public with analysis and information on issues concerning capital punishment. The organization was founded in 1990 and prepares in-depth reports and annual year-end reports, issues press releases, conducts briefings for journalists, and serves as a resource to those working on this issue.

The Justice Project
1025 Vermont Avenue NW, Third Floor
Washington, DC   20005
(202) 557-7584
e-mail: info@thejusticeproject.org
Web site: www.thejusticeproject.org

The Justice Project is a nonpartisan organization dedicated to fighting injustice and to creating a more humane and just world. Founders of the Justice Project are veterans of war who have risked their lives fighting injustice. The Justice Project has worked toward the successful passage of the Innocence Protection Act—the only bipartisan legislation in Congress that addresses flaws in our nation's capital punishment system—which President George W. Bush signed into law on October 30, 2004. It also led the campaign to end the juvenile death penalty. Its monthly newsletter is called the *Criminal Justice Reporter*.

National Coalition to Abolish the Death Penalty (NCADP)
1717 K Street NW, Suite 510, Washington, DC   20036
(202) 331-4090 • fax: (202) 331-4099
e-mail: info@ncadp.org
Web site: www.ncadp.org

Since its inception in 1976, NCADP has been the only fully staffed national organization exclusively devoted to abolishing capital punishment. The NCADP provides information, advocates for public policy, and mobilizes and supports individuals and institutions that support unconditional rejection of capital punishment. Members believe that the death penalty devalues all human life—eliminating the possibility for transformation of spirit that is intrinsic to humanity. The coalition issues a monthly news bulletin called the *National Execution Alert*.

The Sentencing Project
514 Tenth Street NW, Suite 1000, Washington, DC   20004
(202) 628-0871 • fax: (202) 628-1091
e-mail: staff@sentencingproject.org
Web site: www.sentencingproject.org

The Sentencing Project is a national organization working for a fair and effective criminal justice system by promoting reforms in sentencing law and practice and alternatives to incarceration. Founded in 1986, the project has become a leader in the effort to bring national attention to disturbing trends and inequities in the criminal justice system with a successful formula that includes the publication of groundbreaking research, aggressive media campaigns, and strategic advocacy for policy reform. The project issues an annual report and a quarterly newsletter called the *Sentencing Times*.

Bibliography

Books

Stuart Banner — *The Death Penalty: An American History*. Cambridge, MA: Harvard University Press, 2004.

Hugo Adam Bedau — *Debating the Death Penalty: Should America Have Capital Punishment? The Experts on Both Sides Make Their Best Case*. New York: Oxford University Press, 2004.

Stanley Cohen — *The Wrong Men: America's Epidemic of Wrongful Death Row Convictions*. New York: Carroll & Graf, 2003.

David Dow — *Executed on a Technicality: Lethal Injustice on America's Death Row*. Boston: Beacon Press, 2005.

Michael A. Foley — *Arbitrary and Capricious: The Supreme Court, the Constitution, and the Death Penalty*. Westport, CT: Praeger, 2003.

Mark Fuhrman — *Death and Justice: An Expose of Oklahoma's Death Row Machine*. New York: Morrow, 2003.

John F. Galliher — *America Without the Death Penalty: States Leading the Way*. Boston: Northeastern University Press, 2002.

Gary P. Gershman   *Death Penalty on Trial. A Handbook with Cases, Laws, and Documents.* Santa Barbara, CA: ABC-CLIO, 2005.

John Grisham   *The Innocent Man: Murder and Injustice in a Small Town.* New York: Random House, 2006.

Craig Haney   *Death by Design: Capital Punishment as a Social Psychological System.* New York: Oxford University Press, 2005.

Rachel King   *Don't Kill in Our Names: Families of Murder Victims Speak Out Against the Death Penalty.* New Brunswick, NJ: Rutgers University Press, 2003.

Bill Kurtis   *The Death Penalty on Trial: Crisis in American Justice.* New York: Public Affairs, 2004.

Michael J. Martinez and William D. Richardson   *The Leviathan's Choice: Capital Punishment in the Twenty-First Century.* Lanham, MD: Rowman & Littlefield, 2002.

Michael Mello   *Deathwork: Defending the Condemned.* Minneapolis: University of Minnesota Press, 2002.

Joseph Anthony Melusky and Keith A. Pesto   *Cruel and Unusual Punishment: Rights and Liberties Under the Law.* Santa Barbara, CA: ABC-CLIO, 2003.

Erik C. Owens and John D. Carlson   *Religion and the Death Penalty: A Call for Reckoning.* Grand Rapids, MI: Eerdmans, 2004.

Helen Prejean — *The Death of Innocents: An Eyewitness Account of Wrongful Executions.* New York: Random House, 2005.

Irene Quenzler and Richard D. Brown — *The Hanging of Ephraim Wheeler: A Story of Rape, Incest, and Justice in Early America.* Cambridge, MA: Belknap, 2003.

Herman Schwartz — *The Rehnquist Court: Judicial Activism on the Right.* New York: Hill & Wang, 2002.

Eliza Steelwater — *The Hangman's Knot: Lynching, Legal Execution, and America's Struggle with the Death Penalty.* Boulder, CO: Westview Press, 2003.

Scott Turow — *Ultimate Punishment: A Lawyer's Reflections on Dealing with the Death Penalty.* New York: Farrar, Straus & Giroux, 2003.

Jim Wallis — *God's Politics: Why the Right Gets It Wrong and the Left Doesn't Get It.* San Francisco: Harper, 2005.

Franklin E. Zimring — *The Contradictions of American Capital Punishment.* New York: Oxford University Press, 2003.

Periodicals

Steve Basson — "'Oh Comrade, What Times Those Were!'" *Urban Studies* vol. 43, no. 7, 2006.

Thoroddur Bjarnason and Michael R. Welch
: "Father Knows Best: Parishes, Priests, and American Catholic Parishioners' Attitudes Toward Capital Punishment," *Journal for the Scientific Study of Religion* vol. 43, no. 1, 2004.

Michael Cholbi
: "Race, Capital Punishment, and the Cost of Murder," *Philosophical Studies* vol. 127, no. 2, 2006.

Jennifer L. Culbert
: "Why Still Kill? Reconsidering Capital Punishment in the United States," *Political Theory* vol. 32, no. 4, 2004.

Blase J. Cupich
: "How Unconditional Is the Right to Life? Legislators in South Dakota Will Debate Both Abortion and the Death Penalty. How Are the Issues Related?" *America* vol. 196, no. 3, January 29, 2007.

Hashem Dezhbakhsh and Joanna Shepherd
: "The Deterrent Effect of Capital Punishment: Evidence from a Judicial Experiment," *Peace Research Abstracts Journal* vol. 44, no. 1, 2007.

David Garland
: "Capital Punishment and American Culture," *Punishment & Society* vol. 7, no. 4, 2005.

Mark A. Graber
: "From Noose to Needle: Capital Punishment and the Late Liberal State," *The Journal of Politics* vol. 67, no. 1, 2005.

David Johnson and Franklin Zimring
: "Taking Capital Punishment Seriously," *Asian Journal of Criminology* vol. 1, no. 1, 2006.

Chuck Klosterman — "How Old is Too Old to Die? A Few New Wrinkles in the Death-Penalty Debate," *Esquire* vol. 145, no. 4, April 2006.

Ernest W. Lefever — "All Quiet on the Western Front" *Weekly Standard*, February 6, 2007.

Christopher Levy — "Conflict of Duty: Capital Punishment Regulation and AMA Medical Ethics," *Journal of Legal Medicine* vol. 26, no. 2, 2005.

Andrew C. McCarthy — "Trials of This Century: When You Prosecute a Terrorist," *National Review* vol. 58, no. 18, October 9, 2006.

Steven F. Messner and Eric P. Baumer — "Distrust of Government, the Vigilante Tradition, and Support for Capital Punishment" *Law & Society Review* vol. 40, no. 3, 2006.

Mark P. Moore — "To Execute Capital Punishment: The Mortification and Scapegoating of Illinois Governor George Ryan," *Western Journal of Communication* vol. 70, no. 4, 2006.

Patrick Mulvaney — "States Rethink Death Penalty as National Tide Turns," *National Catholic Reporter* vol. 43, no. 20, March 16, 2007.

Paresh Kumar Narayan and Russell Smyth
"Dead Man Walking: An Empirical Reassessment of the Deterrent Effect of Capital Punishment Using the Bounds Testing Approach to Cointegration," *Applied Economics* vol. 38, no. 17, 2006.

Marilyn Berlin Snell
"The Talking Way: In Navajo Country, Traditional Justice, Modern Violence, and the Death Penalty Collide in a Debate Unlike Any in America," *Mother Jones* vol. 32, no. 1, January–February 2007.

Peggy M. Tobolowsky
"Capital Punishment and the Mentally Retarded Offender," *Prison Journal* vol. 84, no. 3, 2004.

James D. Unnever and Francis T. Cullen
"Christian Fundamentalism and Support for Capital Punishment," *Violence & Abuse Abstracts* vol. 12, no. 4, 2006.

James D. Unnever and Francis T. Cullen
"Images of God and Public Support for Capital Punishment: Does a Close Relationship with a Loving God Matter?" *Criminology* vol. 44, no. 4, 2006.

James D. Unnever and Francis T. Cullen
"Reassessing the Racial Divide in Support for Capital Punishment," *Journal of Research in Crime and Delinquency* vol. 44, no. 1, 2007.

Brenda Vogel and Ronald Vogel
"The Age of Death: Appraising Public Opinion of Juvenile Capital Punishment," *Violence and Abuse Abstracts* vol. 10, no. 3, 2004.

Index

Z